Ellin J. Knowles

Spirit and Life

Selections from Bible Readings

Ellin J. Knowles

Spirit and Life

Selections from Bible Readings

ISBN/EAN: 9783337228385

Printed in Europe, USA, Canada, Australia, Japan

Cover: Foto ©Lupo / pixelio.de

More available books at **www.hansebooks.com**

Spirit and Life

Selections from Bible Readings

By

Ellin J. Knowles
(Mrs. J. H. Knowles)

The words that I speak unto you, they are spirit, and they are life.—JOHN 6: 63.

Silver, Burdett and Company
Boston   New York   Chicago
MDCCCXCIX

TO ONE IN HEAVEN
WHOSE COMPANIONSHIP IN
THE STUDY OF THE WORD HAS BEEN
MY INSPIRATION

MIZPAH

"We never used the word while thou and I
    Walked close together in life's working way;
There was no need for it, when hand and eye
    Might meet content and faithful every day;
But now, with anguish from a stricken heart,
    Mizpah! I cry; the Lord keep watch between
Thy life and mine, that death hath riven apart:
    Thy life beyond the awful veil, unseen,
And my poor broken being which must glide
    Through ways familiar to us both, till death
Shall of a surety lead me to thy side,
    Beyond the chance and change of mortal breath;
Mizpah! yea, love, in all my bitter pain,
I trust God keepeth watch betwixt us twain.

"The lips are dumb from which I used to hear
    Strong words of counsel, tender words of praise;
Poor must I go without the cheer
    And sunshine of thy presence all my days.
But God keeps watch my ways and days upon,
    On all I do, on all I bear for thee.
My work is left me though my friend is gone;
    A solemn trust hath love bequeathed to me.
I take the task thy languid hand laid down
    That winter morning, for mine own alway;
And may the Giver of both cross and crown
    Pronounce me faithful at our meeting day!
Mizpah! the word gives comfort to my pain;
I know God keepeth watch betwixt us twain!"

Preface

A FEW selections from the Bible Readings which for fifteen years it has been my privilege to give in many places, are gathered here with the hope that in this more permanent form the precious seed may still be fruitful. Especially to the many hundred women composing the Bible Class of the Young Women's Christian Association of New York, under the care of Miss Ella Doheny, the Chaplain, where for several years it has been my joy to give the Bible lesson on Sunday afternoons, this little book is sent with its glad Easter greeting: "All hail! Peace be unto you."

E. J. K.

Preface

CONTENTS

	PAGE
INTRODUCTION — THE WORD OF A FRIEND, BY BISHOP J. H. VINCENT, D.D.	xi
THE FRIEND OF GOD	1
A SONG OF CONSECRATION FOR THE NEW YEAR	19
THE PRECIOUSNESS OF LOVE	20
BETROTHMENT	51
THE ROYAL COMMISSION	52
HID WITH CHRIST IN GOD	76
GENNESARET	77
THEY CRIED OUT FOR FEAR	88
MORE THAN CONQUERORS	90
THE MOUNTAINEER'S SONG	117
WHAT DO YE MORE THAN OTHERS?	118
EVENING	141
MY CARE	142
HE CARETH FOR ME	155
A LIGHT IN A DARK PLACE	157
A SUMMER BENEDICTION	180

Contents

	PAGE
HIS JEWELS	182
THE HEART'S STORY	212
THINGS WORKING FOR GOOD	213
A DAY OF GOLD	239
UPON MY WATCH-TOWER	240
THE VALLEY OF SILENCE	260
ALL THE WAY	262
RETROSPECTION	286

The Word of a Friend

EASTER DAY is a day of new life—of life from the dead; of life without any foreshadowing of death. The day is full of historic wonder—the wonder of a resurrection from the silence and power of the grave. It is a day full of prophetic promise—the promise of life after death. It is a day full of consolatory assurance—the assurance of a love that death can never extinguish.

As long as we live and love, the wonder, the promise, and the assurance of Easter will give us joy, and Easter lilies will bloom and Easter music fill the air. As long as voices we cherish are stilled by death, and faces dear to us as life itself are hidden in the tomb, we shall continue to be glad because of His coming who added to His words of hope and deeds of healing an actual return from the valley of Silence into the same old world in which He had spoken the words of eternal life.

The words that Jesus spake were His best bequest to the world, and these acquired value from the deeds by which He illustrated and enforced them. He described holiness and lived it. He commended and commanded service—and then Himself served. He told us to give our best to those who need, and then to us gave—Himself. He bade us have no fear of death, and then calmly walked into the realm of death—and came back again. His deeds interpreted and enforced His words. They made History real, and put vital power into Prophecy and Promise.

Easter Day thus puts power into the words of the Holy Book, which we open as Easter lilies bloom about us and Easter bells in the church tower summon us to thanksgiving. What Christ did that first Easter Day makes the Bible to us the Book of Eternal Life. All that the Book teaches of Love and Light, of Peace and Hope, acquires its worth from the fact of the open sepulchre and the ascending Lord.

And it is in this way that the Word of God becomes the medium of Spiritual Life. The Spirit is in the Book, and in the Spirit is Life. And thus are miracles wrought in human lives—even in our times.

In the wonderful poem by Robert Browning, "A Death in the Desert," we have a remarkable illustration of the power of the Divine Word. The aged disciple lay in the innermost cave attended by a few of his chosen friends, who sought, in every possible way, to restore him to consciousness. They dropped wine upon a cloth and chafed his hands. He did not wake. They "broke a ball of nard, and made perfume." He remained silent. "Then Xanthus said a prayer, but still he slept."

" Then the boy sprang up from his knees, and ran,
Stung by the splendor of a sudden thought,
And fetched the seventh plate of graven lead
Out of the secret chamber, found a place,
Pressing with finger on the deeper dints,
And spoke, as 't were his mouth proclaiming first,

'I am the Resurrection and the Life.'
Whereat he opened his eyes wide at once,
And sat up of himself, and looked at us ;
And thenceforth nobody pronounced a word."

Such is the power of the Word which is " Spirit and Life." It contains the seed of immortal blessedness. It has illuminating, awakening, convincing, converting, sanctifying, edifying power.

It is fitting that a loving teacher of the Holy Scriptures should on Easter Day place in the hands of her loyal disciples pleasant reminders of the Book they have so long and so diligently studied.

May this little volume be both " Spirit and Life " to everyone who opens, to peruse, its pages.

JOHN H. VINCENT.

TOPEKA, April, 1899.

SPIRIT AND LIFE

January

The Friend of God

By faith Abraham, when he was called to go out into a place which he should after receive for an inheritance, obeyed; and he went out, not knowing whither he went.

By faith he sojourned in the land of promise, as in a strange country, dwelling in tabernacles with Isaac and Jacob, the heirs with him of the same promise:

For he looked for a city which hath foundations, whose builder and maker is God.—Hebrews 11: 8-10.

THE history and character of Abraham in many respects excel all others in the Bible in interest and in practical lessons for us. Faith is, next to Love, the noblest faculty of the soul. Faith is the groundwork of Love, and without it Love, the sublimest grace of all, can never be enthroned in any human heart. To believe God, as Abraham believed Him, is to be a conqueror over sin, self, and circumstances. It is to live the heavenly life as nearly as it can be lived on earth.

Read the story of Abraham with St. Paul's application of it to the Christian life in the fourth chapter of Romans, and it will make you wise unto salvation.

Abraham had a distinction we may well covet.

Jacob whom I have chosen, the seed of Abraham my friend.—Isaiah 41:8. And the Scripture was fulfilled which saith, Abraham believed God, and it was imputed unto him for righteousness: and he was called the Friend of God.—James 2:23.

Can we possibly reach that distinction ourselves? So then they which be of faith are blessed with faithful Abraham. —Galatians 3:9.

This theme opens so richly, like a vein

The Friend of God

of precious gold or like the farther and farther discoveries of burning planets in the glorious heavens, that I wish we might dwell upon it week after week until its saving truth should be assimilated in our very being. O to learn from Abraham what it means to believe God! To be the friend of God! A friend is one who trusts you—believes in you—will not hear a word against you—stays by you through all vicissitudes — loves you in spite of your faults—will do anything for you—will comfort you—weep with you—rejoice with you—understands you if need be without any explanation. Think of being called the friend of God in a way like that! Not because you are such a saint, nor so distinguished, nor so rich, nor so talented, nor even because you are so much in need of a friend. But because you have that quality which is essential in all friendship,—faith.

There can be no friendship without

faith. You cannot be on terms of intimacy with one you do not believe in, nor with one who does not believe in you. This is not the weak sort of thing we usually mean when we talk of having faith in God. It is more than believing what He says. It is keeping faith with Him in fidelity and constancy, and being so sincere, though perhaps far from perfect, that God can have faith in us, and put confidence in the integrity of our secret soul.

Briefly the story of Abraham,—Genesis twelfth to twenty-fifth chapter.

He dwelt in an idolatrous country. God called him to go into a country of which he knew nothing. He did not tell him the name of the country. He said: "A country which I will afterwards show thee." This was a trial of faith, but nothing compared with the tests which followed it. The more fully Abraham believed and obeyed, the greater the tests became. Lessons are more difficult as we pass into higher classes. It is not a sign of weakness, or of God's displeasure toward us when we are tried to the utmost. Whom the Lord loveth He chasteneth for our profit. Abraham was greatly honored by the tests which God saw he was capable of enduring. So are many of His dearest friends honored now.

When the call came, he obeyed: he went out not knowing whither he went, simply trusting the guidance of God—the God who had promised " I will bless thee and make thee a blessing."

We are going out in the New Year into an unknown country we know not whither. But if only we go believing and obeying as did Abraham, we shall afterward receive it for an inheritance. The promise, " I will bless thee and make thee a blessing," is ours, and every circumstance, every event, every opportunity, disappointment, sorrow, or joy, will be a part of our inheritance, as joint-heirs with Christ; riches laid up unto eternal life. What a vast inheritance the New Year offers if only we believe and obey!

It is encouraging to know that Abraham's was not a perfect faith. He was exactly like us, and if we could read between the lines in this simple biography we would see how his faith was a growth cultivated by circumstances, by providential leadings, by discipline and trial. But it grew to its stalwart proportions, so that he is called the Father of the Faithful, because he obeyed. The path of obedience is always the path of progress in the life of every human soul. His faith faltered, and he was led into serious mistake and danger when he went into Egypt and said what was not true about Sarah, his wife.

There is so much that is suggested, not written, in all these charming Bible stories. The romance of love, old as

Eden, is retold again and again. Sarah, a beautiful woman, won Abraham's heart in the early days. And while much that does violence to the standards of our own times appears in the story, yet through all, the golden thread of a pure love runs distinctly: one woman's power over the heart of one man. Pure human love does not interfere with friendship with God.

Sarah was always queen of Abraham's life, no matter who else appeared upon the scene. She understood the true feminine art of government, so it is said of her that she " obeyed Abraham, calling him lord." Every true woman feels that sort of respect for a man whom she can admire and trust, and is glad to yield deference to him if his character is such as commands it.

But at the same time Sarah evidently had her own way when she set her mind upon it. The story tells us how, when once again Abraham's faith faltered because he could not see how God could perform His promise to his seed while he had no son, Sarah proposed a plan of her own—(you must read it in Genesis 16)—and like all human plans which are formed in impatience at God's delays, it brought her into serious trouble. But "Abraham hearkened to the voice of Sarah": "one touch of nature makes the whole world kin." Yet, like the long-suffering and forgiving God that He is, after this God spoke to Abraham, renewing His covenant, and told him that Ishmael, the son of the bondwoman, was not to be the heir of the promise, but Sarah's son.

Here surely was a trial of faith far beyond anything which had yet tested Abraham. What! he one hundred years old, and Sarah ninety!

Abraham, the father of us all (as it is written, I have made thee a father of many nations), before Him whom he believed, even God, who quickeneth the dead, and calleth those things which be not as though they were. Who against hope believed in hope, that he might become the father of many nations, according to that which was spoken, So shall thy seed be. He staggered not at the promise of God through unbelief; but was strong in faith, giving glory to God; And being fully persuaded, that what He had promised He was able to perform. And therefore it was imputed to him for righteousness. Now it was not written for his sake alone, that it was imputed to him; But for us also, to whom it shall be imputed, if we believe on Him that raised up Jesus our Lord from the dead; Who was delivered for our offenses, and was raised again for our justification.— Rom. 4: 17–25.

For twenty-five years the fulfillment of this promise was delayed. It is not written, but doubtless many, many times the question arose, "Am I mistaken? Have I misunderstood the Lord? Am I presumptuous to believe a thing so contrary to nature and to all precedent? Has God forgotten?"

Ah! we know that sometimes even the faith of Abraham, under discipline, needed the added assurance of the word of God. He said: What wilt thou give me seeing I go childless? I see no sign of the fulfillment of Thy word. Then God said: Fear not, I am thy shield and thy exceeding great reward. Look now toward heaven and tell the stars, if thou be able to number them: so shall thy seed be. And he believed in the Lord; and He counted it to him for righteousness.—Genesis 15: 1-6. So that a man shall say, Verily there is a reward for the righteous: verily He is a God that judgeth in the earth.—Psalm 58: 11.

God is a rewarder of them that diligently seek Him.—Hebrews 11: 6. For what saith the scripture ? Abraham believed God, and it was counted unto him for righteousness. Now to him that worketh is the reward not reckoned of grace, but of debt. But to him that worketh not, but believeth on Him that justifieth the ungodly, his faith is counted for righteousness. Even as David also describeth the blessedness of the man, unto whom God imputeth righteousness without works, Saying, Blessed are they whose iniquities are forgiven, and whose sins are covered. Blessed is the man to whom the Lord will not impute sin. Cometh this blessedness then upon the circumcision only, or upon the uncircumcision also ? for we say that faith was reckoned to Abraham for righteousness. —Rom. 4: 3-9. And that was counted unto him for righteousness unto all generations for evermore.—Psalm 106: 31.

In the eighteenth chapter of Genesis, 1-5, we find interesting suggestions as to the relation a friend of God bears to others. His mission is to comfort hearts.

Every friend of God is doing this, whatever else he leaves undone. Three strangers came by Abraham's tent, and with the readiness of habitual courtesy he said, "Rest yourselves under the tree." The word really means "lean ye down." O how good for tired hearts it is for some friend of God to say "Lean ye down"! Let the tension relax. Let me share your burden. Let me refresh you, you are so tired. "Stay" your hearts, the word really is. Only a friend of God can be a "stay" to other hearts. The soul that leans and rests against Love and Strength omnipotent, can hold up others. That is one of the blessed privileges a friend of God has. It is worth while to bear all manner of testing to reach a point where we can truly comfort hearts. Nor did Abraham speak as though he thought he was doing some great thing in this kindness. He said, Let me give you a little water and a morsel of bread, when all the while he meant to give them the very best he had; "for therefore are ye come to your servant."

So it was ordered of God that these men should come to him not so much that they might get what he would give, but that he might have the opportunity to serve them. The friend of God, he recognized that opportunities to do good and to minister to others are favors sent to us, not favors given. I think it is Phillips Brooks who says the world cannot be divided into benefactors and beneficiaries. The one who has the means and the opportunity to give is as much the beneficiary as the one who receives.

Another privilege of friendship is open-heartedness with no concealment of thoughts or plans. Shall I hide from Abraham that thing which I do?—Genesis 18:17. Jesus says: Henceforth I call you not servants; for the servant knoweth not what his lord doeth: but I have called you friends; for all things that I have heard of my Father I have made known unto you.—John 15: 15.

Abraham, in communion with God, knew the destruction that was coming upon Sodom; Lot, in Sodom, knew it not. Many shall be purified, and made white, and tried; but the wicked shall do wickedly; and none of the wicked shall understand; but the wise shall understand. —Daniel 12: 10.

The friend of God can plead with Him for others. "Abraham stood yet before the Lord." Every request was granted. Sodom would have been spared if ten good people could have been found in it, and Lot was saved through Abraham's prayer. The world owes much to the prayers of the friends of God. We have ourselves been shielded, comforted, prospered, because some trusted friend for

The Friend of God

years has talked with Him about us every day.

But perhaps Abraham's height of faith and friendship seems beyond our little possibilities. Do not be discouraged. Abraham grew; so may we. " The righteousness of God is revealed from faith to faith," and is " imputed to them who walk in the steps of that faith of our father Abraham." He went step by step, not by great leaps. The man whose faith has been deeply tested and who has come off victorious, is the man to whom supreme tests must come. The finest jewels are most carefully cut and polished; the hottest fires try the most precious metals. Abraham would never have been called the Father of the Faithful if he had not been proved by uttermost trials.

Read Genesis, twenty-second chapter: " Take thy son, thine only son, whom thou lovest "! At every stroke the Lord cut deeper into the heart of His friend, on the cleavage line of his dearest treasure.

"It is such an apparently unreasonable demand. It is so unlike God. He cannot mean it. I could not love a God who would require such a thing of me."

So we say in the presence of mysteries which baffle our faith. But not so Abraham. He who had been tested often, who had been obedient, who had always proved God true if he waited God's time, could meet a trial which would have overthrown a soul less closely in fellowship with God.

See him going with a chastened, wistful, yet humbly obedient heart up Moriah's height, with the idol of his heart beside him about to be sacrificed at the command of a God whom he had faithfully loved and served! What a rebuke to our questionings of God's dealings with us! Away with all doubting explanations of this stupendous scene! It was an object-lesson for the ages. Angels were looking. Shall this man's faith stand forever for the strength and help of all God's people? Shall it be known through him that unfaltering faith will always prove the faithfulness of God? Yes; and when faith had borne victoriously its uttermost test, the angel of the Lord—who? the Lord Jesus, Jehovah, He in whom "all the promises of God are yea and amen "—spoke to him, saying, " Now I know that thou fearest God." Thou hast trusted me to the uttermost. I will also trust thee; thou shalt ever be called my friend, and I will bless thee and make thee a blessing; in thee shall all nations be blessed. It is always so, and always will be: " they that are of faith are blessed with faithful Abraham."

That the trial of your faith, being much more precious than of gold that perisheth, though it be tried with fire, might be found unto praise and honor and glory at the appearing of Jesus Christ.—1 Peter 1: 7.

Great things are in store for the Lord's tried and true friends at His "appearing."

There is touching pathos in the simple statement, Abraham came to mourn for Sarah and to weep for her.—Genesis 23:2. The friend of God is in sorrow; but we know that Jesus wept with His friends in Bethany. When he was old and well stricken in age, it is said, " The Lord had blessed Abraham in all things," and he "died in a good old age, an old man, and full" (Genesis 25:8). Not full of years, but himself full; a good old age; satisfied, happy, contented; such an old age as only the friends of God know. He was gathered to his people, and Jesus lifts the veil of the unseen (Luke 16), and shows us His friend with the angels, still "comforting" another friend, Lazarus, who has just come out of earthly trials into the glorious company of heaven. Blessed is it indeed, in time and eternity, to be the friend of God!

A SONG OF CONSECRATION, FOR A HAPPY NEW YEAR.

The bells of my heart are ringing,
    Happy bells!
Ringing a shout of thanksgiving,
Ringing a pæan of praise;
Up to the skies doth the melody rise,
This happiest day of my days.

The bells of my heart are ringing,
    Thankful bells!
For the Spirit reveals this truth to me:
That wholly unworthy though I may be,
A wonderful price has been paid for me,
And therefore, my Lord, I belong to Thee.

The bells of my heart are ringing,
    Grateful bells!
This is the song of their musical chime:
Lord, I am Thine, entirely Thine,
Thy name is written on all I call mine,
For all eternity and for all time.

Ring on, ring on, sweet spirit bells!
    Blessed bells!
Ring on forever, and nevermore cease,
In my inmost being, your chimes of peace.
Ring joyful peals! for this day so blest,
Dawns on my soul her Sabbath of rest.

                          E. J. K.

February

The Preciousness of Love

Beloved, let us love one another: for love is of God; and every one that loveth is born of God, and knoweth God.—1 John 4:7.

ST. JOHN, who wrote more about love than any other of the disciples, learned its preciousness and came into the possession of it through intimacy with Jesus. In his youth he was ambitious to sit in a place of power at the right hand of the Lord in His kingdom, the favorite of the King. Jesus told him then that such a place was not a gift; it must be won by the person who shall hold it, and as He asked the searching question, Can ye drink of my cup, and be baptized with my baptism of suffering? He revealed the price of that high posi-

The Preciousness of Love

tion, — love, self-forgetful, self-renouncing love.

Men and women are striving to see who shall be uppermost; who shall be most admired, most praised, most powerful. Jesus taught His ambitious disciple that the greatest among men was he who loved most, and did most to make the world better and happier. "Even as the Son of man came not to be ministered unto but to minister, and to give His life a ransom for many." At another time John saw a man casting out devils and forbade him because he was not one of the company of Jesus' disciples. He was narrow and exclusive, he could not rejoice in the good done by one who did not follow just the methods he approved. Jesus taught him a broader charity when He said, " He that is not against me is for me."

At another time, when the Samaritans would not permit the Lord to pass through their villages, John, furious with resentment, asked, " Shall we call down fire on them from heaven as did Elijah ? " Jesus promptly rebuked him, saying, " You know not what spirit you are of." This is not my spirit, this is not love. I came to save men, not to destroy them. But companionship with Jesus changed all this. Closer and closer his intimacy grew until he became distinguished as the disciple whom Jesus loved, who leaned upon His bosom and shared His secret thoughts.

One wrote upon a frosted pane the words God, Love, Home. Were these all ? Did they comprehend everything sweet and pure and lovely ? Indeed, are there not too many already ? Yes; home means love; only two words were left; God and Love. Too many yet, for God is Love. So on a new pane was written the one word, God. That comprehended all.

The Preciousness of Love

How much is enfolded in that one little word of four letters, Love! Take the flower of your life—all that makes up that unseen but real thing which we call our life, and from root to outermost leaf love is its essential part. You may pick it in pieces as you would a rose, tear off petal after petal of the immortal blossom, and you find love written on all, and in its very heart the stamina and strength of all is love. Fancy your life bereft of love.

Love is the one sole comfort left for sorrowing, burdened humanity amid the wreck which is our inheritance from the fall. The Arch-Fiend, whose very essence is the opposite of love, would fain have despoiled us of all good. But the Cherubim and flaming sword, mystical emblems of the highest manifestation of Love, the Redemption in Christ Jesus, were placed where they "kept," or guarded and preserved, the way to the Tree of Life. It was not wholly lost;

the love of God in Christ is kept as a door of hope for His disobedient and misguided children. For He loved us from the foundation of the world, and has set Himself from the beginning to save humanity as far as possible from the evil designs of the Adversary, and to restore to all who will accept it finally, through Infinite Love, all that was lost. Herein is love; not that we loved God, but that He loved us, and sent His Son to be the propitiation for our sins.—1 John 4: 10.

All love is of God. Love, wherever you see it, is the nearest like God of anything in all the universe. St. John was only stating a fact of human experience when he said, " He that loveth not, knoweth not God." Nothing is so far from fellowship and acquaintanceship with God as an unloving heart. And on the other side, " He that loveth, knoweth God, for God is love."

The Preciousness of Love

Even on the lowest plane of spiritual apprehension, it is true that pure human love brings God within our comprehension more than anything else can, except the direct revelation of Him through the Holy Spirit. The more power of unselfish loving we possess, the more like God we are, for God is love. I believe a study of love, human love and divine love—the one is a gleam and glimmer of the other,—a study of it as this blessed Book presents it to us, and as human experience exemplifies it, will bring us nearer to God. He uses human affection to illustrate His own Divine Heart.

Can a woman forget her child? Yea, they may forget, yet will I not forget thee. Behold, I have graven thee on the palms of my hands.—Isaiah 49: 15, 16.

A mother was told she had only a few hours to live. " I must live until Johnnie comes," she said, and mother-love, stronger than death, held the silver cord until the boy for whom she had prayed through years of wandering came back to promise he would follow his mother's Saviour.

If a son shall ask bread of any of you that is a father, will he give him a stone ? Or if he shall ask an egg, will he offer him a scorpion ? How much more shall your heavenly Father give the Holy Spirit to them that ask Him ?—Luke 11 : 11–13.

As the bridegroom rejoiceth over the bride, so shall thy God rejoice over thee.—Isaiah 62 : 5. Prepared as a bride adorned for her husband. Come hither, I will shew thee the Bride, the Lamb's wife.—Revelation 21 : 2, 9. The Spirit and the Bride say, Come.—Revelation 22 : 17. Husbands, love your wives, even as Christ also loved the church, and gave Himself for it.—Eph. 5 : 25.

Beloved, let us love one another, for love is of God. I never saw that simple

The Preciousness of Love

affirmation before as I see it now. All the love that makes your life worth the living, the love of husband, mother, sister, brother, and friend, the sweet affection of that darling child whose soft arms will twine around your neck this evening, all the love that you prize as life's dearest possession, is of God. It came from nowhere else. It is His gift, born of His own heart; proof of His own eternal love. We have taken it as a thing of course, and call it natural affection. But who made the nature capable of loving; who sowed the seeds of love close by the fountain of life in your heart ? Beloved, let us love. Let us do nothing to drive this sweet dove of peace and blessing from our homes or our hearts.

Love is of God, and "where love is there God is." We cannot afford to wound by negligence, unkindness, or want of reciprocity, so dear, so precious a thing as love. Many waters cannot quench love, neither can the floods drown it: if a man would give all the substance of his house for love, it would utterly be contemned.—Song of Solomon 8:7.

I read this beautiful incident in a New York daily paper: "My Darling." These words in bright letters stood out in bold relief on the dashboard of a huge four-horse truck in a Broadway blockade. The driver looked as unsentimental as possible, but he was not profane or brutal toward his horses. Patiently he waited the loosening of the jam, while his neighbors filled the air with curses. Finally, his horses becoming restive, he climbed down from his box and soothed them with gentle words and caresses. Then a bystander asked why he called his truck "My Darling." "Why," he said, "because it keeps the memory of my daughter, little Nellie. She's dead now, but before she died she clasped her arms around my neck and said: 'Papa, I'm

The Preciousness of Love

going to die, and I want you to promise me one thing, because it will make me so happy. Will you promise?' 'Yes,' I said, 'I'll promise anything. What is it?' Then, fixing her eyes on mine, she said: 'Oh, Papa, don't be angry, but promise me you'll never swear any more, nor whip your horses hard, and be kind to mamma.' That's all there is about it, mister, but I promised my little girl, and I've kept my word." When the blockade was lifted, the big truckman resumed his seat, and was soon lost in the tide of travel. Will anyone say this is not of God?

There is nothing so touching as the exhibitions of love among the poorest and roughest classes of humanity. Those who visit among the poor, and see homes destitute of every comfort, mothers worn out with care and hunger, and little children with the merest supply of life's bare necessities, could give many illustrations of the softening, refining, heavenly influences of love. Wherever we find it, let it be henceforth more than ever sacred to us, for love is of God.

It surprised the shiners and newsboys around the Post Office the other day to see "Little Tim" coming among them in a quiet way and to hear him say: "Boys, I want to sell my kit. Here's two brushes, a hull box of blacking, a good stout box, and the outfit goes for two shillings." "Goin' away, Tim?" inquired one. "Not 'zactly, boys, but I want a quarter the awfullest kind just now." "Goin' on Skursion?" asked another. "Not to-day, but I must have a quarter," he answered. One of the lads passed over the change and took the kit; and Tim walked straight to the counting-room of a daily paper, put down the money, and said, "I guess I kin write if you give me a pencil."

With slow-moving fingers he wrote a

The Preciousness of Love

death notice. It went into the paper almost as he wrote it, but you might not have seen it.

He wrote: "Died, Litul Ted, of Scarlet fever; gone up to Hevin, left one brother." "Was it your brother?" asked the cashier. Tim tried to brace up, but he could n't. The big tears came up, his chin quivered, and he pointed to the counter and gasped, " I—I had to sell my kit to do it, b—but he had his arms around my neck when he d—died." He hurried away home; but the news went to the boys, and they gathered into a group and talked. Tim had not been home an hour before a barefoot boy left the kit on the doorstep, and in the box was a bouquet of flowers which had been purchased in the market by pennies contributed by the crowd of ragged but big-hearted boys. Did God ever make a heart which would not respond if the right chords were touched?

This story too is told in a daily paper:
"You sha'n't have it! I won't give it up!" A very old and forlorn-looking woman had been arrested for vagrancy in the streets of a great city. She was dirty, ragged, and miserable. Her brown and wrinkled face wore a distressed and weary look. Her bony fingers closed tightly over something held in her right hand, thrust under her ragged apron. "You sha'n't have it!" she said, angrily, to the officer whose duty it was to search prisoners before confining them in their cells. "Let me see what it is, anyhow," he said half coaxingly. "It aint anything you'll want," she said, drawing back, with her hand still hidden in the folds of her apron. "It aint anything I can do any harm with. It's just a little kind of a—a—keepsake." The old woman began to cry, with her arm held over her eyes. "You'll have to let me look at it," said the officer, kindly but firmly; "it's the

The Preciousness of Love 33

rule of the prison. You may keep it, perhaps, after I 've seen it." The wrinkled hand came slowly out from under the apron, the bony fingers were unclasped, and there in the shivering palm lay a ragged little shoe. "Pshaw! I don't care for that," said the officer, a little huskily. "I knowed you would n't," sobbed out the woman; "but I care a good deal for it. It 's a keepsake, you know."

A keepsake; the one little bond between the life that was and the life she knew; a tiny remnant of the happy past, clung fondly to in the sorrowful present. "It was my baby's shoe, his first and only one," she said. "I 've carried it thirty-five years, and I 'd have been a worse woman 'n I am now if it had n't been for that little shoe." There was no proof that she was a bad woman now. Unfortunate she surely was, and the world had not been kind to her. Vagrants have hearts and souls. That ragged little shoe had for all those years been the treasure and the comfort of the one; it may have been the salvation of the other. It may have been her shield against temptation, her strength in hours of weakness, her consolation amid all the sorrows of her hard life; and in the end, it might lead the helpless old soul to the cross of the Christ who had carried her babe in His bosom, and whose arms were outstretched toward herself.

> " Whatever is mighty, whatever is high,
> Lifting men, lifting women, their natures above,
> And close to the kinship they hold in the sky,
> Why, this I affirm—that its essence is Love."

In a prison in Massachusetts is a man on life sentence. He has shown a desperate spirit ever since he came in, and has twice plotted a general outbreak in the prison, but has been discovered. Since then, he has obeyed orders, but with a sullen spirit. Last June a party of strangers visited the prison. With them were two little children. The guide took one of the little girls in his arms to carry her up-stairs. This man, moody and sullen, stood near. "Jim," said the guide, "won't you help this other little girl up the stairs?" He scowled. The child held out her hand: "If you will, I guess I'll kiss you." His scowl vanished; he lifted her tenderly as a father would. Half-way up the stairs she kissed him. At the head of the stairs she said, "Now, you've got to kiss me too." He blushed, looked into her innocent face, kissed her cheek, and went down the stairs with tears in his eyes. Ever since that day he has been a changed man. Maybe somewhere he has a little one of his own; no one knows, for he never tells his past life, but the change so quickly wrought by that loving kiss proves that he may yet be a saved man.

"Down in the human heart
Crushed by the tempter,

> Feelings lie buried that grace may restore.
> Touched by a loving hand,
> Wakened by kindness,
> Chords that are broken may vibrate once more."

Beloved, let us love one another, for love is of God. Let us love men and women into hope and salvation.

The Lord hath appeared of old unto me, saying, Yea, I have loved thee with an everlasting love: therefore with lovingkindness have I drawn thee.—Jeremiah 31:3. The drawing power of love; loved thee from the pit, drawn thee out by love. Only by love will God draw all men unto Himself.

Every one that loveth is born of God, and knoweth God. Love, then, is the revealer of God. He that loveth me shall be loved of my Father, and I will love him, and will manifest myself unto him. If a man love me, he will keep my words: and my Father will love him, and we will come unto him, and make our abode with him.—John 14:21–23.

The Preciousness of Love

If this faint, crushed rose of human love at which we have been looking, set about by many a thorn, yet so sweet that despite its thorns, which prick us often so sorely, we count it the most precious thing in human existence; if this imperfect yet so blessed treasure is of God, what must be that great divine heart, that reservoir of eternal, infinite love, from which these sweet streams flow? *In this was manifested the love of God toward us, because that God sent His only begotten Son into the world, that we might live through Him. Herein is love, not that we loved God, but that He loved us, and sent His Son to be the propitiation for our sins.*—1 John 4:9, 10. *But God commendeth His love toward us, in that, while we were yet sinners, Christ died for us.*—Romans 5:8.

Greater love hath no man than this, that a man lay down his life for his friends.—John 15:13. *For God so loved the* world, that He gave His only begotten Son, that whosoever believeth in Him should not perish, but have everlasting life. For God sent not His Son into the world to condemn the world; but that the world through Him might be saved.—John 3: 16, 17. Beloved, if God so loved us, we ought also to love one another. No man hath seen God at any time. If we love one another, God dwelleth in us, and His love is perfected in us. Hereby know we that we dwell in Him, and He in us, because He hath given us of His Spirit.—1 John 4: 11-13. His spirit of love, not only love for those who love us, but His spirit of love for everybody.

Everyone that loveth is born of God. Not everyone that loveth some person, or some thing, not love that has a selfish element in it, as most human affection has, but everyone that loveth with the broad, unselfish love that reaches to the unlovely, to those who do not love us in

The Preciousness of Love

return, who do not expect our love, the great, sinful, suffering humanity. Everyone who loves this way is born of God, for such love comes only through being made a partaker of the divine nature, in a high, spiritual sense. He that loveth not in this broad and Godlike measure knoweth not God, for God is love. If a man say, I love God, and hateth his brother, he is a liar. And this commandment have we from Him, That he who loveth God love his brother also.—1 John 4: 20, 21.

Love, then, love to God, and love to all our fellows, is the supreme good, the fulfilling of the law. Then one of them, which was a lawyer, asked Him a question, tempting Him, and saying, Master, which is the great commandment in the law? Jesus said unto him, Thou shalt love the Lord thy God with all thy heart, and with all thy soul, and with all thy mind. This is the first and great commandment. And the second is like unto it, Thou shalt love thy neighbor as thyself. On these two commandments hang all the law and the prophets.—Matthew 22: 35-40.

Read the 13th chapter of 1 Corinthians over and over and over again.

And now abideth faith, hope, love, and the greatest of these is love. Yes, " the greatest thing in the world."

Above all things have fervent love among yourselves: for love shall cover the multitude of sins.—1 Peter 4: 8. Hatred stirreth up strifes: but love covereth all sins.—Proverbs 10: 12.

Love suffereth long. So patient to serve, and wait, and watch; and is so kind; so careful not to wound, but rather to take the thorns and sharp stones out of every path. Envieth not; so glad to see another happy and prosperous. Is not puffed up. Esteems others better than itself, in sweet humility of mind.

The Preciousness of Love

Doth not behave itself unseemly; is never rude, or discourteous, or disagreeable. Seeketh not her own. Nothing is so unselfish as true love. Is not easily provoked. It takes something of consequence to make love angry; unselfish love is not disturbed by trifles; it is good-tempered. Rejoiceth not in iniquity, but rejoiceth in the truth. It is trustful, sincere, looks on the bright side, and is far more ready to believe the good than the evil that is said of its friends and acquaintances. What a blessed state of society would we have if love ruled!

How shall we get this sweet angel of all good to dwell in us? God is love; he that dwelleth in love dwelleth in God, and God in him.—1 John 4:16. Make a way for God to come, by cultivating a loving spirit through loving deeds. The best way to please God is to be kind to some of His other children. Love grows by use, as other attributes of the mind and heart grow. "I shall pass through this world but once. Any good thing, therefore, that I can do, or any kindness I can show to any human being, let me do it now. Let me not defer it, for I shall not pass this way again."

Jesus always made much of love, more than of anything else, because it is the root and essence of all good living and working.

"Simon, lovest thou me?" He asked. "Her sins, which are many, are all forgiven, for she loved much," He said of Mary. A loving heart compels to service, and in the last day love will be the final motive by which we shall be judged. For unto those who love Him He will say, "I was an hungered and ye fed me." To those whose love was so little that it never saved them from a selfish life, He will say, "Ye did it not to me." Shall it be said of us,

The Preciousness of Love 43

" I lived for myself, I thought for myself,
  For myself and none beside,
Just as if Jesus had never lived,
  As if He had never died "?

Not only if God so loved us ought we to love one another, but how should we love Him who first loved us. The Life of Bishop Selwyn says: In the early days of Sister Dora's nursing mission at Walsall, she had achieved a wonderful success in saving for a workingman his arm. The limb had been so terribly mangled by some machinery that the surgeons decided it must be amputated. But the poor man's groans and expressions of despair went to the nurse's heart; and when he appealed to her, " Oh, Sister, do save my arm for me, it's my right arm," with a swift glance she took in the possibilities of the case, and determined to try. Her skill and attention were rewarded with success; and the patient installed himself as one of her most devoted admirers, calling to inquire for her when she was ill, and begging the portress to "tell Sister it was her arm that rang the bell."

In the same way as Sister Dora, at her Cottage Hospital at Walsall, Bishop Selwyn once saved an arm. In visiting a hospital, he met on the steps a dejected-looking figure with a sentence of death from the doctors ringing in his ears. For he had positively refused to allow his arm to be amputated, and was preparing to take the consequences. "I 'd a deal rather die, sir; and I 'm going home to tell my wife so. I could n't bear to live, just to be a hobble on her and the children."

The Bishop's sympathy was enlisted on behalf of the poor man, and arrangements were at once made for sending him to a London hospital. Some time afterward, the happy, grateful convalescent appeared at Litchfield and asked to see the Bishop. With great pride and

The Preciousness of Love

satisfaction he pulled up his sleeve and showed him his arm. It was almost well and already in a fair working condition, owing to the insertion of a silver tube in place of the diseased bone which had been removed. "It's the Bishop's arm now for ever, if he wants it," said the man, enthusiastically, and he showed it to several lookers-on; "a five-pound note he paid down to give me my silver arm, and it's just the same as his arm now." Ye are not your own; ye are bought with a price: therefore glorify God in your body, and in your spirit, which are God's. —1 Cor. 6: 20.

> " O, love of God, how strong and true !
> Eternal, and yet ever new ;
> Uncomprehended and unbought,
> Beyond all knowledge and all thought."

So sang one who has now entered into fuller comprehension of eternal love. By a flash of light from the ever blessed Spirit, who takes of the things of Christ and shows them unto us, while yet in the flesh, he saw how wondrous is the unbought love of Him who gave His life for us. In the clearer light of heaven, with the open vision of the Father's face, what would he say now of that love? O if we could but hear! O if we could but hear from any of those we have known who have gone where they know even as they are known, I think they would say:

"Dear friend, let me tell you how it used to seem to me when I was where you are, and how it seems to me now. Well do I remember the doubts and anxieties that filled my heart; how the uncertainties of the future stretched like dark shadows over the way. How lonely I felt. How unequal to life's work and burdens. How I questioned the love and care of God. How wrong the appointment of my lot appeared. Ah, dear heart, I remember well those experiences of my earthly life. But how little I knew!

The Preciousness of Love

How very much clouded was my sight by the mists of the world! It is all so different now. Looking back, I see I never was alone. I never was left to uncertainty. I never had any work given me, nor any burden put upon me, without adequate strength given. And oh! the love of God so strong and true, so tender and watchful, even when I doubted it. If you could only know that love as I know it now, you would go on with a courage and calmness that nothing could move. Believe that love, dear friend. You cannot believe it too much; you cannot trust it too far; you cannot frame any language that could express what we, in heaven, know of the eternal love of God."

But while the voices we have loved cannot speak to our mortal ear, the Infinite Lover Himself speaks so plainly that we must understand. Hear Him saying: I have loved thee with an everlasting love; Greater love hath no man than this, that a man lay down his life for his friends. As the Father hath loved me, even so have I loved you. Behold, I have graven thee upon the palms of my hands. I will not leave you comfortless. Even the very hairs of your head are all numbered. Not a sparrow falleth to the ground without your Father; fear ye not, therefore, ye are of more value than many sparrows.

What then? Would we take the testimony of a saint in heaven as more assuring than the word of God Himself? Surely no. We need no voice other than His to quiet every misgiving and send us forward with calm and confident step.

Whatever comes, let us know and believe the Love. We can walk courageously through darkness when Love goes with us. We can bear disappointment when Love has the management of our affairs. We can endure pain when Love soothes us and says, " It is but for a moment." We can stand before the iron doors of great mysteries without fear when we know Love holds the key.

O, thou unknown future, before whose portal we stand blind and deaf to all thou may'st have in store for us, we cross thy threshold with undaunted step, for we are persuaded that neither life, nor death, nor things present, nor things to come, shall be able to separate us from the love of God which is in Christ Jesus our Lord. Beloved, if God so loved us, we ought also to love one another, so that good deeds, kind deeds, helpful, loving acts and words may flow out to all around us, the far away as well as the near.

" Like a cradle rocking, rocking,
　Silent, peaceful, to and fro,
Like a mother's sweet looks dropping
　On the little face below—

Hangs the green earth, swinging, turning,
    Jarless, noiseless, safe and slow ;
Falls the light of God's face, bending
    Down and watching us below.
And as feeble babes that suffer,
    Toss and cry, and will not rest,
Are the ones the tender mother
    Holds the closest, loves the best ;
So when we are weak and wretched,
    By our sins weighed down, distressed,
Then it is that God's great patience
    Holds us closest, loves us best !
O great heart of God ! whose loving
    Cannot hindered be, nor crossed,
Will not weary, will not, even
    In our death itself, be lost.
Love divine ! of such great loving
    Only mothers know the cost,
Cost of love, which all love passing,
    Gave a Son, to save the lost ! "

BETROTHMENT.

And I will even betroth thee unto me in faithfulness, and thou shalt know the Lord.—Hos. 2 : 20.

"Lovest thou me?" O Saviour of my soul,
   Thou readest here Thine answer in my heart ;
All its deep pulses leap to Thy control,
   Responsive to Thy whisper, " Mine thou art."

How could it be that I should love Thee not,
   When I such revelations have of Thee?
Thy character, surpassing human thought,
   Thy wondrous love, so tender unto me.

And yet I grieve Thee! O Thou Christ adored!
   I bow before Thee weeping in the dust ;
Canst Thou forgive the thoughtless act and word,
   The heart that fails to yield Thee all its trust?

O love, that bears so much! All symbols fail—
   Mother and lover, husband, brother, friend,
The dearest earthly ties can never tell
   Love's deepest meaning without change or end.

From Thy dear hand the pledge divine I take,
   The token given only to Thine own ;
The name Thou callest me for love's sweet sake,
   The secret written in the pure white stone.

O blessed union ! where with open face,
   With steadfast gaze, Thy glory I can see ;
Till, by the precious mysteries of grace,
   I change in likeness, Lord of love, to Thee.

E. J. K.

March

The Royal Commission

As Thou hast sent me into the world, even so have I also sent them into the world.— John 17 : 18.

THESE are wonderfully suggestive words, spoken in the prayer of Jesus to the Father, for His disciples, and repeated to them after His resurrection. As my Father hath sent me, even so send I you.—John 20: 21. How was Jesus sent into the world, and for what purpose? As a royal messenger he came from the royal household. God, who at sundry times and in divers manners spake in time past unto the fathers by the prophets, hath in these last days spoken unto us by His Son.—Heb. 1 : 1, 2.

Can it be that you and I have any

right so to dignify our mission in life as to compare it with that of our Lord and King? O Christian, do you comprehend your privilege as a child of the royal blood, partaker of the divine nature, partaker of the heavenly calling, the high calling of God in Christ Jesus? The mission which He came from heaven to fulfill is verily the mission of His followers.

Ye are a chosen generation, a royal priesthood, an holy nation, a peculiar people; that ye should show forth the praises [or virtues] of Him who hath called you out of darkness into His marvelous light.—1 Peter 2:9.

It is a grand and noble thing to live. Let us feel that we are sent into life with a purpose, and for a purpose; life can then never lose its interest, never become under any circumstances utterly dull and commonplace.

For none of us liveth to himself, and no man dieth to himself. For whether we live, we live unto the Lord; and whether we die, we die unto the Lord: whether we live therefore, or die, we are the Lord's. —Rom. 14: 7, 8. And for every soul that belongs to Him He has use and a place. Fear not, I have redeemed thee; I have called thee by thy name; thou art mine.—Isa. 43: 1. So we do ourselves a great wrong if ever we sit down in the shadow of our own gloomy thoughts, saying, as Jonah did, " It is better for me to die than to live." That need not be true of anyone. It is our own fault if it is true; there must be use for us as long as God bids us stay here.

We are sent upon the same mission as that of the Lord Jesus. The Spirit of the Lord is upon me, because He hath anointed me to preach the gospel to the poor; He hath sent me to heal the broken-hearted, to preach deliverance to the captives, and recovering of sight to the blind, to set at liberty them that are bruised, to preach the acceptable year of the Lord.—Luke 4 : 18, 19.

"I wonder how you can endure to go into those vile places and sit beside those unclean people and talk to them," said a woman to another who was accustomed to do such work as is described in ,the verses just quoted. "I thought that was what Christians were for," was the quiet reply. So it is; this is their mission everywhere they go; and above all they are sent to fulfill it in their own homes. Go down to thine own house and show what great things God hath done unto thee.—Luke 8 : 38. If we cannot show it there, in our manner and spirit, we may be sure we need better preparation before we try to show it elsewhere.

We are to fulfill our mission in the Spirit of Jesus. Whosoever will be chief among you, let him be your servant. Even as the Son of man came not to be ministered unto, but to minister.—Matt. 20:27, 28. Let nothing be done through strife or vainglory; but in lowliness of mind let each esteem other better than themselves. Look not every man on his own things, but every man also on the things of others. Let this mind be in you which was also in Christ Jesus.—Phil. 2:3-5.

We must do our work for others in the spirit of love and compassion. God sent not His Son into the world to condemn the world, but that the world through Him might be saved.—John 3:17. How do we feel toward those not so fortunate as ourselves? Do we feel aversion, or pity and desire to help? The spirit of "Stand thou aside for I am holier than thou," never yet helped another. Truly may we say, as we look at a fallen brother or sister, "There goes myself but for the grace of God."

And the disciple, like the Master, is "anointed" for service.

The Royal Commission

Ye shall receive power after that the Holy Ghost is come upon you: and ye shall be witnesses unto me.—Acts 1:8. And, behold, I send the promise of my Father upon you. . . . All power is given unto me in heaven and in earth, go ye therefore. And lo, I am with you alway unto the end of the world.

The commission is personal. I have not your mission to fulfill, nor you mine. The Son of man is as a man taking a far journey, who left his house, and gave authority to his servants, and to every man his work.—Mark 13:34. Whatever our sphere, it gives it both dignity and interest to feel that it did not come by chance, but is ours by divine appointment.

These words are very suggestive in their connection with our Lord's assurance that he would soon return from that "far journey." He has not given us our work and then lost His interest in it. He is coming back to give it personal inspection, and to bestow upon each one a " reward according as his work shall be."

It is said of us, as Christians, that " we are His workmanship, created in Christ Jesus unto good works, which God hath before ordained that we should walk in them." What must we think, then, of a Christian who feels no responsibility for anything beyond personal salvation? who, if a brother or sister be naked, or destitute of daily food, either bodily or spiritual, gives them not those things which are needful?

> " If suddenly upon the street
> My gracious Saviour I should meet,
> And He should say : ' As I love thee,
> What love hast thou to offer me?'
> Then what could this poor heart of mine
> Dare offer to that heart divine?

> " His eye would pierce my outward show ;
> His thought my inmost thought would know,
> And if I said, ' I love Thee, Lord,'
> He would not heed my spoken word,
> Because my daily life would tell
> If verily I loved Him well.

> "If on the day or in the place
> Wherein He met me face to face
> My life could show some kindness done,
> Some purpose formed, some work begun,
> For His dear sake, then it were meet
> Love's gift to lay at Jesus' feet."

The necessity for work—" by the sweat of thy brow shalt thou eat bread "—we associate with the curse of sin, but like many another thing in which we misunderstand our good and loving God, instead of being a part of the curse, it is one of His benevolent ways of relieving the consequences of man's sin. How one pities the people who stand around with nothing to do! What a boon is good hard work to humanity! Many a man or woman is saved by it from hopeless depression of spirits, and saved, too, from crime, for " Satan finds some mischief still for idle hands to do."

What is true of work for mankind in general is eminently true of Christian service. It is a blessing. It gives healthful exercise to the powers of mind and heart. Many a one has been saved from (unwholesome introspection,) from the consuming fire of unhappy thoughts, through the occupation of some benevolent or religious work; and many have been saved, too, from the currents of worldly society by having the hands and the time filled by the pressing demands of the various charities and missionary organizations. Do we call it a sacrifice of self to engage heartily in these things? Rather let us call it a great privilege, one of God's favors toward us, for the enrichment of personal character and the unfolding of the best energies of the soul.

And the honor of being a co-worker with Him! Who shall estimate that? There is no place for discouragement in any truly Christian work. It must succeed. There are no words sufficiently expressive for this thought: " Sow in the morning thy seed, and at evening withhold not thy hand, for thou knowest not which shall prosper, whether this or that, or whether both shall be alike good." There is no intimation of the possibility that either morning or evening sowing can be bad.

There are some conspicuous hinderances to the doing of our work, through which many Christians are standing all the day idle, and, of course, losing their reward. One is want of courage. They are afraid to follow their best convictions because of the criticism of those who observe them. They "love the praise of men more than the praise of God." Nothing but a supreme love to God, which makes us value His approval above everything else, will overcome this hinderance.

Another hinderance is a false humility. "Because I can do so little, or cannot do it as well as others, therefore I will do nothing. I will never be missed from the ranks of the workers because my influence is so small; my words would have but little weight, therefore I may as well be silent." Such humility is close of kin to pride. True humility says: "I can do all things through Christ which strengtheneth me." Forgetting self, trusting in Jesus, is the secret of successful service.

Self-indulgence is one of the chief hinderances to usefulness. We mean to find some work; indeed, we have found it; but it costs effort. It requires some sacrifice of ease to teach a Sunday-school class, to be a parish visitor, to undertake some reform in the household, to fill our place in the prayer-meeting, and so on through all the golden line of opportunity. What shall raise us from our selfish indifference? The one remedy, the one inspiration, is to realize in the depths of a loving and grateful heart this truth, "that Christ died for all, that they which live shall not henceforth live unto themselves, but unto Him which died for them, and rose again," and to say with the heartiness of a sincere devotion, "Whose I am, and whom I serve." A living branch of the True Vine cannot cease from doing that which Jesus says glorifies the Father: "Herein is my Father glorified, that ye bear much fruit."

In that picture of the glorious future of the Church in Revelation, 22d chapter, there is the Tree of Life, bearing twelve manner of fruits, and yielding her fruit every month for the healing of the nations. The Tree of Life is the Lord Jesus Christ, and branches of that tree should be like Himself, fruitful always for help and healing.

At the Beautiful Gate of the Temple once a lame man lay. Peter and John spoke to him, and the man looked earnestly at them, "expecting to receive something from them." This man was like hundreds that we meet every day.

They are looking at us, Christians, expecting to receive something from us. And they have a right to expect it. We have meat to eat that they know not of, and their hungry hearts should get help from us. We have riches they have no share in; it is a shame if we pass them by without at least a little gift from our abundance. Peter said to the lame man: "Silver and gold have I none, but such as I have give I thee." He was only fulfilling the spirit of that practical word of St. Paul: "As every one hath received the gift, even so let him minister one to another, as good stewards of the manifold grace of God."

So we have only to give " such as we have." But what " manifold grace " is ours to share with others! As we rest by the seashore, or revel in mountain air, or wander over green fields where the temptation will be to think we have no responsibility of fruit-bearing for the time, what opportunities will come to us to be " good stewards of manifold grace "! A word in season to one that is weary; an expression of appreciation to some hard-working man or woman; consideration for those who serve us; the " lend-a-hand " spirit toward all we meet, whether it be in spiritual or temporal affairs—all these will be occasions wherein we may " glorify our Father."

There is one sort of work of which there is so much to do that the Lord has given it to a large majority of His disciples. It is His own kind of work, and in it we find sweet fellowship with Him. It is *patient continuance*. Sometimes we think it stands in the way of everything, and does not count for anything. " Just patient continuance in one round of duty, when I might be accomplishing so much if I only could have a little change!" But Paul says, Who will render to every man according to his deeds: To them who by patient continuance in well doing seek for glory and honor and immortality, eternal life.—Rom. 2:7. Men may get glory and honor in other ways, but they never can get more than the patient continuer in well doing will have—eternal life, which comprehends all that the infinite God can give.

There is a procession passing my window, and how much more those men in line are doing than they know! They are putting down with their steady, martial step an old truth with new emphasis for me. It would not be much of a parade if it were made up only of the band and the men in uniform. Of course, these attract attention, but, after all, the ranks that follow, each man in his place keeping step, make up an array which is worthy to be called a procession.

This, then, is my lesson for the day. I have only to march on, keeping step with my Leader, and, although I wear no

The Royal Commission 67

distinguishing uniform nor sound a drumbeat for recognition, yet my place is important, and the life-ranks will miss me if I ignobly drop out before I am regularly dismissed by my General in command.

We are apt to think only of the distinguished workers when considering the great movements of the age. The head of a manufacturing establishment is the embodiment of that interest in our eyes; but how long could his engines move or his looms weave without the workmen, each in his place? We look at a picture and think only of the artist; how could his ideal have found expression had not the unknown artisan prepared the canvas, fashioned the brush, and mixed the paints?

There are passages of Scripture we often overlook which have in them a blessed lesson for us if we will search it out. For instance, 1 Chronicles 4: 23: "These were the potters, and those that dwelt among plants and hedges: there they dwelt with the king for his work."

How could the king have had a palace with lovely surroundings if there had been no potters and gardeners in his household? Surely it was not by accident the names of these men were written in the Book. The Holy Spirit would teach this lesson, so needful for us who are so often discouraged, and so ready to discount as useless the commonplace service of every day, that the appointed task and the appointed place, however seemingly insignificant, are just as important as any others, and just as blessed, too, if only we *dwell with the King for His work.*

There is no joy upon earth sweeter than the joy of ministering to others. In one of those times of intercourse with His disciples, when Jesus said many things which have never been written, but which left an influence upon their hearts which we feel as we read what they have written concerning Him, He said: "It is more blessed to give than to receive." St. Paul reminded the people of this word of Jesus. He must have been told it by one of the twelve who heard Him say it; and by his own life of self-forgetful service he proved the truth of the saying.

In all His teaching the Lord Jesus unfolded eternal principles. He was not arbitrary or dogmatic in His doctrine. He did not affirm in the Beatitudes that certain persons were blessed because He would have it so, but because in the nature of things it was so. Men might try every way possible to their imagination to be blessed, but they never could arrive at the goal they sought except through the seven beautiful gateways of the Beatitudes. Just so He taught that to be greatest and happiest among men is to be as He Himself was among them, "as one that serveth." Not because He arbitrarily lays down a law that he who would be greatest must be servant of all, but because in the very constitution of things, in the constitution of God Himself, the law is essential and eternal. Unselfish loving, unfailing outpouring of kindness and beneficence, have always made the joy of heaven; and wherever these qualities most fully possess human hearts, there earth is nearest like heaven.

It is not then a matter of regret that we live in a day when great demands are made upon our time, our sympathy, our means, for the helping of the needy. We may well be thankful for the privilege.

Who can tell what bearing our training here in the sweet ministries of love may have upon our capabilities to be God's messengers of blessing in the hereafter? We do not know what He may have for His redeemed people to do in the eternities. No lagging years of inglorious ease are they! But years of glad service without weariness, with larger capacities, with

The Royal Commission 71

clearer vision, with the perfection of joy of which we have now a little foretaste, as we follow Him who went about among the common people doing good.

There is danger perhaps, in the great pressure of things to do, in our many charities of this day, that we may lose the real blessedness of ministering. Just so soon as we get, like Martha, cumbered with much serving, the very sweetest charities become a drudgery. We have seen exceedingly careworn-looking persons rushing from committee to committee, from entertainment to lecture, for "sweet charity's sake," heavily laden with tickets, weary with responsibility, laboring over the problem as to whether the project on hand will " make " or " lose " for the treasury.

It is a question if such ministering is very "blessed." Sincere it is, doubtless; and far be it from us to underrate the real, unselfish service rendered in these ways by most efficient workers in all our boards of charities. But why lose the sweetness of the service in the hurry and rush of performing it? If we must needs be on many committees, the making of which there seems to be no end, let us keep the blessedness in the dullest routine by remembering another word of the Lord Jesus, how He said: "For whosoever shall give you a cup of water to drink in my name, *because ye belong to Christ*, verily I say unto you, he shall not lose his reward." That motive always in view may lift even the selling of tickets above the commonplace, and keep the soul serene amid the tumult of committees.

There is a sweet and suggestive story called "The Cup of Loving Service." A boy stood shading his eyes with his little hand, gazing up the steep, rough road which wound about a mountain. Behind him was a small house set in a patch of grass and garden, with every sign of pov-

The Royal Commission 73

erty, yet with evidences of carefulness and content. From a peg in the shed adjoining the house, the boy took a pewter mug, a tin pail and cover, and a coarse clean cloth from the next nail, and hastening to a spring near by he filled his pail with the clear, cool water, covering it carefully from the hot, noontide sun.

Then he bound the cup to the belt at his waist and began the toilsome ascent of the mountain. Presently he found a traveler, overcome by fatigue and heat, prostrate upon the ground. Taking some cool water in his cup, he pressed it to the fainting lips. Revived by the draught, the traveler asked, " What angel of mercy sent you to mé, child, in this forsaken wilderness ? How did you know I was weary and thirsty ? Give me another cup; never was draught so sweet!" And then he offered his little succorer a coin.

The boy drew back. " O no, sir," he said; " this is the cup that mother says is without money and without price, and although we are very poor, sir, God has been so good to us; for He has given us a beautiful spring which is always running beneath the rock right by our home, and mother says we must always feel so thankful for it, and we must not forget the verse somewhere in the Bible which says, ' Freely ye have received, freely give.' O no, sir, I could not take your money. You see, this is the cup of loving service, mother says, and we must fill it and share it with those who pass by and are very tired and thirsty. If you will look at it, you will see what mother wrote upon it a long time ago."

"Yes, child, I can read the words, ' Ready for loving service in the name of Christ.' Child, suppose the spring should cease to flow?"

"How could we do without the spring, and the cup never lifted down and filled? But oh, I am sure the spring will always run, sir," eagerly answered the boy. We cannot here follow farther this beautiful story of loving service; but may not our hearts be like this little, homely, useful cup, always bearing the inscription, " Ready for loving service in the name of Christ," filled every day afresh from the fountain of living waters, the eternal love of God, carrying refreshment to many a weary traveler along the steep and rugged roads of human life. " As the Father hath sent me into the world even so send I you."

HID WITH CHRIST IN GOD.

Wait, my impatient soul! come thou and rest
   In the deep quiet of thy Father's heart;
The rush and tumult, and the chafing toil
   Have wearied thee; come to this "place apart."

Remember how thy Saviour's patient soul
   Was vexed with this same world that wearies thee,
And how He said, when human helpers failed,
   "Yet not alone; the Father is with me."

Come, hide with Him, companionship most dear;
   'T will be for thee to dwell with Christ in God—
To enter with Him the most holy place,
   Where only those He leads have ever trod.

And yet, strange paradox, though hidden here,
   Still thou must keep thy place in outward strife;
Hidden with Christ means fellowship with Him
   In bringing this sad world to light and life.

The needs of men shall press thy soul, as His,
   But sight is clearer in this place apart;
A calm, expectant faith will nerve thy toil,
   Hidden with Jesus in the Father's heart.

Come, tired soul! the worry and the fret
   Make life and service seem a heavy load!
Leave them outside—come, find that toil is rest,
   In this sweet hiding-place, *with Christ in God!*

E. J. K.

April

Gennesaret

And straightway Jesus constrained His disciples to get into a ship, and to go before Him unto the other side, while He sent the multitude away.—Matthew 14 : 22.

And He saw them toiling in rowing; for the wind was contrary unto them: and about the fourth watch of the night He cometh unto them, walking upon the sea, and would have passed by them.—Mark 6 : 48.

Then they willingly received Him into the ship: and immediately the ship was at the land whither they went.—John 6 : 21.

THIS little inland sea, so often crossed and recrossed by our Lord and His disciples, the scene of so many miracles, is suggestive as a symbol of human life. What a variable area it was! Now quietly sleeping in the embrace of precipitous hills, reflecting the soft clouds by day and the watching stars by night; then tossed into unreasoning fury in a moment by the sudden rising of the passionate winds. Ships of adventure, pleasure, or traffic were constantly passing over it, and many times it carried on its waves Christ and His Church, the hope of humanity through coming ages; and once and again would that little Church have been wrecked had not the divine Leader been near to succor and save.

There was one occasion when He sent His few disciples away to do His bidding, seemingly without Him. It appears from the narrative that they went reluctantly, but Jesus constrained them.

It was dark; evening had come; there may have been signs of storm, and it seemed as if there must be reason why they should stay and relieve the Lord of that great multitude who were thronging Him after the miracle of the loaves and fishes. But notwithstanding their unwillingness to go, and the apparent reasons for staying, He constrained them to get into the ship, while He attended to the multitudes and then went alone into a mountain to pray.

They seemed to go without Him, yet how near He was! Never once did He lose sight of that boat, and, better still, He never lost control of it. The darkness deepened on the sea, the waves tossed the ship at their mercy, and the great wind that blew was contrary. Jesus saw them. Darkness never hides anyone from Him. He saw them distressed in their efforts to resist the storm; they were doing all they could, but they not only made no headway, but were in peril of their lives. And yet He waited. It was the fourth watch of the morning before He came to them walking on the sea. Three o'clock—that time before dawn when things seem at their worst; that hour when flesh and heart fail, and we think we cannot toil in rowing any more, but must let the ship sink — then He comes, walking on the waves we thought would overwhelm us.

But He does not enter the ship yet, nor even speak. It seems as though He would pass by without a word. Why? Surely it was to show them He had control; that no waves were so high that He could not walk above them, and that they, too, were safe in a storm with Him.

But their faith was not yet equal to this. They all saw Him, but, instead of being calmed by His presence, they were troubled; they did not know Him. But Jesus would not suffer their faith to be tested above that they were able, so immediately He talked with them and said: "Be of good cheer: it is I; be not afraid." Then they willingly received Him into the ship, and immediately they were at the place whither they went.

So He tests our faith. So He sends us out upon a sea He knows will be stormy. So He lets us toil against head winds. So it sometimes seems as if He would pass by us in our extremest peril without a word. But He never forgets; He never ceases to watch; He never fails to come at the right moment; He never fails to speak good cheer to the souls fainting with fear; He never fails, when we willingly receive Him into our heart and life, to bring us safely out beyond the storm into His present and eternal peace.

We are sent out into life without our own choice; sometimes to occupy a place or do a work quite against our will.

And Moses said unto the Lord, O my Lord, I am not eloquent, neither heretofore, nor since Thou hast spoken unto Thy servant: but I am slow of speech, and of a slow tongue. And the Lord said unto him, Who hath made man's mouth? or who maketh the dumb, or deaf, or the seeing, or the blind? have not I the Lord? Now therefore go, and I will be with thy mouth, and teach thee what thou shalt say. And he said, O my Lord, send, I pray thee, by the hand of him whom Thou wilt send. — Exodus 4: 10–13.

But God's eye is upon every little boat on life's sea. Neither is there any creature that is not manifest in His sight: but all things are naked and opened unto the eyes of Him with whom we have to do.— Hebrews 4: 13.

He is master of every situation. Ah Lord God! behold, Thou hast made the heaven and the earth by Thy great power and stretched out arm, and there is nothing too hard for Thee. Behold, I am the Lord, the God of all flesh: is there anything too hard for me?—Jeremiah 32: 17, 27.

He could have come sooner to their relief upon Gennesaret, but He waited. For

Gennesaret

as the heavens are higher than the earth, so are my ways higher than your ways, and my thoughts than your thoughts.—Isaiah 55 : 9.

For I know the thoughts that I think toward you, saith the Lord, thoughts of peace, and not of evil, to give you an expected end.—Jeremiah 29 : 11.

Just when they were ready to say, " We can toil no longer," He came.

There hath no temptation taken you but such as is common to man: but God is faithful, who will not suffer you to be tempted above that ye are able; but will with the temptation also make a way to escape, that ye may be able to bear it.—1 Cor. 10 : 13.

He seemed to pass by without caring. So He waited until Lazarus died before coming to His friends in Bethany. He said, " I am glad I was not there, to the intent ye may believe." Jesus could calm the sea, or He could walk above the tempest. "He maketh the clouds His chariots."

Who are kept by the power of God through faith unto salvation ready to be revealed in the last time. Wherein ye greatly rejoice, though now for a season, if need be, ye are in heaviness through manifold temptations: that the trial of your faith, being much more precious than of gold that perisheth, though it be tried with fire, might be found unto praise and honor and glory at the appearing of Jesus Christ: whom having not seen, ye love; in whom, though now ye see Him not, yet believing, ye rejoice with joy unspeakable and full of glory.—1 Peter 1 : 5–8.

When their faith failed He spoke: "Be of good cheer: it is I; be not afraid." So He comforts us by His Word in the trials of our faith.

These things I have spoken unto you, that in me ye might have peace. In the

Gennesaret

world ye shall have tribulation: but be of good cheer; I have overcome the world. —John 16: 33.

When they knew Him, they willingly received Him.

I am the good shepherd, and know my sheep, and am known of mine. My sheep hear my voice, and I know them, and they follow me.—John 10: 14, 27.

The purpose of life is fulfilled when we take Jesus into our hearts and lives. For all things are yours. Whether . . . the world, or life, or death, or things present or things to come; all are yours; and ye are Christ's; and Christ is God's.— 1 Cor. 3: 21-23.

" My bark is wafted on the strand
 By breath divine ;
And on the helm there rests a Hand
 Other than mine.

" One who was known in storms to sail,
 I have on board :
Above the roaring of the gale,
 I hear my Lord.

"He holds me when the billows smite—
    I shall not fall;
If sharp, 't is short; if long, 't is light—
    He tempers all.

"Safe to the land! safe to the land!
    The end is this;
And then with Him go hand in hand
    Far into bliss."

There is a picture of this scene upon Gennesaret by one of the masters. The storm is high; the boat is helpless; the men on board lift imploring hands. Peter starts to walk to Jesus, but begins to sink. The face of Jesus is calm; He knows the storm is under His control. *Immediately* He stretches out His hand to Peter. There is no loss of time when His disciple is in real danger. He catches him. Peter is not holding Jesus; the firm grasp of omnipotence is upon Peter's arm in answer to his cry for help. There is no need for both of Jesus' hands. One is enough. The other is raised with the question, "O thou of little faith, where-

Gennesaret

fore didst thou doubt?" It was in a moment of ecstatic faith that Peter started to walk the waves. Looking to Jesus, he was above them; looking at the waves, he began to sink. Which was the true life? The moment of faith, or the moment of doubt?

O strong and mighty Saviour, O dear and blessed Friend! Wherefore do I doubt?

"THEY CRIED OUT FOR FEAR"
(Matt. 14 : 26).

Lord Jesus, I would not fear Thee
   Could I see Thee walking the sea;
'T is light on the boisterous billows
   When I know Thee coming to me.

Lord Jesus, the wind is heavy,
   The stars are gone out from the sky;
Over the voice of the tempest
   Let me hear Thee say, " It is I."

Jesus, my spirit is broken,
   Nor longer can breast the strong waves;
O reach forth Thy hand and catch me,
   Thy right hand which comforts and saves!

Come, Lord, as once in the night watch
   To toiling disciples of old;
Surely it is for my comfort
   Gennesaret's story is told.

Lord, I have toiled all the night long—
   Thou hast reason, I know, for delay—
But 't is the fourth watch, Lord Jesus,
   O tarry no longer, I pray!

Casting off all that could hinder,
   I would walk the waves to Thy side,

Gennesaret

But, Lord, my faith does not measure
 The rushing and merciless tide.

Stretch forth Thy hand and deliver,
 And chide me, my Lord, if Thou will ;
Shame for me, Jesus, to doubt Thee,
 Yet doubting, O pity me still !

Open my eyes to behold Thee,
 Let me know Thee coming to me.
I would not fear Thee, Lord Jesus,
 Could I see Thee walking the sea.

E. J. K.

May

More than Conquerors

In all these things we are more than conquerors through Him that loved us.—Romans 8:37.

"A WINNER in life's battle,"—these were the words which held my gaze and stirred my soul's depths as I read a brief sketch of one whom I knew and loved years ago, and who had just entered upon her reward. A winner in life's battle—how true! I think of the peculiar trials of that life, and the rich, strong, helpful character of the woman who made even the trials minister to her highest success, never conquered by them, and I say, Yes—a winner indeed! More than a conqueror she. She carried away in her victorious grasp very much spoil.

How much richer is the world for the life of such a woman! How many through her influence and example have learned the secret of victory!

"We brought nothing into this world, and it is certain we can carry nothing out." This is true, indeed, of all material possessions. My hands may be full of silver and gold to-day. My possessions, as men count possessions, may be the envy of others less fortunate. But to-morrow these same hands may lie empty and helpless; the silver and gold with all that it can purchase—except as it ministered to higher things—belongs to another. I can carry none of it out. But do I take nothing with me? Ah, yes; the character I have gained, whatever sort it is, is my possession forever. Then

How much better is it to get wisdom than gold, and to get understanding than silver?—Proverbs 16: 16.

We must see from the Word, if we

read, how intrinsically valuable every one of us is in the sight of God, and how the chief aim of Him who made and redeemed us is to bring each of us to the best and highest possible development. If we can only realize that to be happy and comfortable is not the chief end of life, but that to be strong and true and pure—in a word, like Him who is "the chiefest among ten thousand, the one altogether lovely"—is the highest end of our being, we would stop looking for the easy places, and hiding away from all the discomforts, and mourning over the enemies to our progress. For, like the enemies of Israel, they are bread for us.—Numbers 14:9.

We gain strength through our difficulties, and carry away very much spoil from every well fought battle.

And Asa and the people that were with him pursued them unto Gerar: and the Ethiopians were overthrown, that they could not recover themselves; for they were destroyed before the Lord, and before His host; and they carried away very much spoil.—2 Chronicles 14: 13.

The strength that comes from difficulties met and overcome is well worth all that it costs.

There is in all of us a secret longing and in most of us a distant hope that some day we shall realize the meaning of the word victorious. The thought of victory rings through our souls like the peal of far-off bells, suggestive and sweet to the ear as it floats over hill and valley and through heavy mists, yet so far away that we cannot hope to reach the temple whence the glad sound comes, or to sit ourselves with the happy worshipers. Victory ? Ah, yes, for others, but not for me. I go about with such a humiliating consciousness of defeat that sometimes even the hope of a victory that shall have any permanence dies out of my heart. Most of my days are begun with the expectation of conquering, but alas! the evening song is too often in the minor key and the refrain is:

> " Fever and fret and aimless stir,
> And disappointing strife,
> All chafing, unsuccessful things,
> Make up the sum of life."

And judging from my present ill-success the hope of final overcoming is dim. I do not give it up altogether, for sometime I hope to be victor, but the joy of that hope is all gone out of me. I fail to have the earnest of it now.

But, beloved, the gospel of the word to-day is the victor's song.

Nay, but in all these things we are more than conquerors through Him that loved us.—Romans 8: 37.

Not that I speak in respect of want: for I have learned in whatsoever state I am, therewith to be content. I know both how to be abased, and I know how to abound: everywhere and in all things

I am instructed both to be full and to be hungry, both to abound and to suffer need. I can do all things through Christ which strengtheneth me. — Philippians 4:11-13.

Shall I talk of defeat, of being led captive, of being the servant of sin or of circumstances, when I can be more than a conqueror?

Know ye not that to whom ye yield yourselves servants to obey, his servants ye are to whom ye obey.—Romans 6:16.

For sin shall not have dominion over you.—Romans 6:14.

He will turn again, He will have compassion upon us; He will subdue our iniquities; and Thou wilt cast all their sins into the depths of the sea.—Micah 7:19.

That He would grant unto us, that we being delivered out of the hand of our enemies might serve Him without fear, in holiness and righteousness before Him all the days of our life.—Luke 1:74, 75.

Stand fast therefore in the liberty wherewith Christ hath made us free, and be not again entangled in the yoke of bondage.—Galatians 5 : 1.

We have a fashion of looking at other Christians and saying: " Oh, I suppose they never had trials such as I have. They have not the same nature to contend with. They can talk of trusting God, because they have nothing to try their faith. They can talk sweetly of forgiving their enemies, because they have nothing to forgive; everybody is good to them; they can be good, because they have nothing inside or outside to make them anything else. But it is not so with me; beset on every side with peculiar trials, hampered by a peculiar temperament, hedged up as nobody ever was before." It would be a curious study if the inner life of one could be uncovered to another! What surprises we would meet! How ashamed some of us would be of our misjudgments of others, and of our own murmurings against circumstances! We would see how some among us who have reached a place of quiet victorious faith have really climbed there, pricked by many a thorn, struck by many a falling rock, encompassed by many an obscuring fog, yet have climbed through all to a blessed, heavenly outlook beyond the clouds, which more than repays all the cost of climbing. We would see the feet that seem so strong and steady have come through weary, devious ways, stumbling often, and faltering at many a point. We would see the hearts most at rest have come to it through the stormiest experiences. We would see struggles going on this moment in many hearts where we least suspect it; and, more than all, we would see that those who seem the strongest in faith and Christian principle are most conscious of weakness, and are leaning hard and close upon the Divine

Heart, conquerors " through Him " always, their watchword: " Not I, but Christ." The blessed book does not say, " He that has an easy time and gets through life with the least trouble shall inherit all things." But it does say, "He that overcometh shall inherit all things."

He that overcometh, the same shall be clothed in white raiment; and I will not blot out his name out of the book of life, but I will confess his name before my Father and before His angels.—Revelation 3 : 5.

Him that overcometh will I make a pillar in the temple of my God, and he shall go no more out: and I will write upon him the name of my God, and the name of the city of my God, which is new Jerusalem, which cometh down out of heaven from my God: and I will write upon him my new name.—Revelation 3 : 12.

To him that overcometh will I grant to

sit with me in my throne, even as I also overcame, and am set down with my Father in His throne. He that hath an ear, let him hear what the Spirit saith unto the churches.—Revelation 3: 21, 22.

To him that overcometh will I give to eat of the tree of life which is in the midst of the paradise of God.—Revelation 2: 7.

Of course, all these promises to him that overcometh imply something to be overcome. And after all, though we think we have so much to hinder, and such a hard fight to gain the mastery, it is a good thing for us to have the contest. We shall be victors if we find out the secret of overcoming, and we never could become this if we had never had the enemy to meet.

We glory in tribulation also, knowing that tribulation worketh patience; and patience, experience; and experience, hope.—Romans 5: 3, 4.

What graces of true character are here, all inwrought and brought to perfection through tribulation! That word means pressure, squeezing—a harrow. Life is made up of little things. The squeezing comes that way, the every-day trials press us most. The way we meet them goes very far toward making up character. The conflict and the conquest are not so much outside as within, in the hidden realm of the soul. Victory here means victory everywhere. Self-conquest is kingship. One has said: "Patience is a beautiful grace to look at, but a desperately hard one to live." St. James says: "Let patience have her perfect work, that ye may be perfect, entire, wanting nothing." So then, "desperately hard" though it may be, it surely is worth the effort, if to gain this grace is to be "perfect, entire, wanting nothing." We are told by the blessed Master, in whom this lovely grace, amidst sorest provocation, was so luminous, that we are to "hear the word, keep it, and bring forth fruit with patience." How seldom do we see fruit or flower brought forth in perfection the very day the root or seed is planted! Have patience, then, with yourself, discouraged friend. If the true seed is in the heart, nourish it, and patiently expect the fruit. "For ye have need of patience, that after ye have done the will of God, ye might receive the promise."

O that I might be patient! But how can I be, with all the worry and rush of these days! Ah! these are just the things that cause this charming grace to grow. They are intended for that purpose, though seemingly so adverse. "Knowing that tribulation worketh patience." The little annoyances, the friction that "rubs the wrong way," are the elements in which patience may most thrive. Who ever became patient when everything went well? The most blessedly patient soul I know is one whose daily squeezing and harrowing have been exceptional.

St. Paul tells us to be " gentle unto all, apt to teach, patient." We are more " apt to teach," as a rule, than to be the other thing. " Why cannot those children remember what I tell them ? " said a father in an irritated tone. It is well for parents to consider how many times they forget their Father's word to them, and how patient He has been through all the years.

How shall we gain this crowning grace ? Not of ourselves alone, but through Him who is able to strengthen us " with all might, *according to His glorious power*, unto all patience and long-suffering with joyfulness."

He that is slow to anger is better than the mighty, and he that ruleth his spirit than he that taketh a city.—Proverbs 16: 32.

Ah indeed! If your own spirit—your self—is overcome, conquered, then you know what it is to be enriched with the spoils of victory.

> " Finding, following, keeping, struggling,
>   Is He sure to bless?
>   Saints, Apostles, prophets, martyrs
>   Answer, ' Yes.' "

Jesus overcame His enemies by silence.

And Jesus stood before the governor: and the governor asked Him, saying, Art Thou the King of the Jews? And Jesus said unto him, Thou sayest. And when He was accused of the chief priests and elders, He answered nothing. Then said Pilate unto Him, Hearest Thou not how many things they witness against Thee? And He answered him to never a word; insomuch that the governor marveled greatly.—Matthew 27: 11-14.

And the chief priests accused Him of many things: but He answered nothing. —Mark 15: 3.

Set a watch, O Lord, before my mouth: keep the door of my lips.—Psalm 141: 3.

If any man offend not in word, the same is a perfect man, and able also to bridle the whole body.—James 3: 2.

If you covet strength and beauty of character, begin now to be more than conquerors in the every-day difficulties, within and without. We are either victors or captives. Life is a struggle. If we enter the kingdom of heaven at all we enter through much tribulation. If it does not come in outward trial, it does come in the inner life of the soul. No Christian life is vigorous and fruitful that knows nothing of conflict. To float with the stream is not to float to broad and deep experience; we float toward the shallows. If we are making real progress, Satan will put in our way many hinderances; if he does not, there is good reason to think he sees nothing to fear for his kingdom from us. It is the stanch fighter he resists.

The powers of the mind, like the muscles of the body, become strong and adapted to certain lines of action by use. It is not easy for one whose daily thought is concentrated upon business pursuits to go into deep lines of spiritual contemplation. The easy thing to do is to suffer the mind to flow on in the well worn channels; it is like turning water-courses upward to set the current toward the higher and the heavenly. What then? Must the stream of true life sink away from sight in the meadows and lowlands, or shall it be so richly fed from the springs of God's eternal heights, that it shall make even meadows and lowlands fertile? The Saviour said we must *strive* to enter into life eternal. He assures us that the kingdom of heaven, " which is righteousness, peace, and joy in the Holy Ghost," is never found in the natural course of

things, but " the violent take it by force."
We need a great deal more of the athletic
in our religion. While we cry " Halt!"
in the rush for place and power and wealth
in worldly things, we cry in spiritual
things, " Awake, put on thy strength!"

If the pressure of earthly care makes the
spiritual sense dull of apprehension, let
us somehow or other, by whatever effort
it may cost, " enter into our closet *and
shut the door*," and get an audience with
God, which will be heard by Him and by
ourselves as well. If the appetite for
spiritual food is languid, let us insist
upon taking the pure milk of the word
until the healthy hunger of the soul returns.

We are careful to use means to
strengthen our bodies when weak; why
not use like wisdom in the treatment of
the spirit? There are certain exercises
of the soul which have great effect to
brace its weakness and bring us up to

good spiritual health. They are recommended by the Great Physician. One is this: "Love your enemies; do good to them which hate you; and pray for them that despitefully use you." This is a sort of exercise we would rather see used by others than ourselves. It is not easy doing, as we know if we have tried it in downright practical earnest. But it does mightily toughen the spiritual muscle!

We do not believe in the old ascetic doctrine of self-inflicted discipline. But we do believe there are forms of self-denial in many ways which are good for spiritual exercise, and we are in danger of hearing the Master say, "Come unto me and rest," more clearly than we hear the same voice saying, "If any man follow me, let him take up his cross daily and come after me." Strong meat, says St. Paul, is for those who, by reason of use, have their senses exercised to discern both good and evil. Oh, how the world needs Christians of this sort, who can and do eat "strong meat," and have clear discernment because of the sturdy use of their spiritual senses!

The overcoming of every-day trifles leads up to the strength for greater victories. No one was ever fitted for large responsibilities who suffered herself to be conquered by little worries, or appalled by common tasks. Hetty Ogle, in the telegraph office at Johnstown, saw the flood rushing toward her with angry haste, but firmly she stood at her post, doing the present duty, sending messages of warning over the wires, thereby saving many lives, though her own life paid the price of theirs. It was seeming defeat for her, for not a trace was ever found of her bruised and perhaps burned body. But her noble spirit, what of that? We count her among our heroines to-day, but she did not become a heroine in a moment. Her life from early girlhood had been one of self-discipline and constant overcoming of obstacles, and in this supreme moment the heroic character, which was the growth of years, shone with immortal luster.

A woman of refinement by the force of circumstances was compelled to live out in the wilds near a coal-mine. She was grandly more than conqueror of her uncongenial surroundings by her cheerful acceptance of the situation; and by devoting herself to the welfare of the miners' families she "carried away much spoil" in their gratitude and in the good she did.

A young Christian girl was always present at the prayer-meeting, but sometimes it was at the expense of her mother's comfort and strength, because her help was needed in the home. It was revealed to her by the Holy Spirit that what she had supposed was faithful religious service was pure selfishness. It was hard: but she met it fairly; looked it full in the face, as every accusation of conscience should be met. She said to her mother: "I have been selfish; if you will forgive me I will try to have a more Christian spirit." She hung this motto up in her room:

"Content to fill a little space,
If Thou be glorified."

In her daily life since then it is even more apparent to others than to herself that she carried off much spoil from that victory.

A young woman, serving as kitchen-maid, was so discontented with her lot that she grew morose and ungracious, and lost all her Christian joy. A friend led her to see how wrong her spirit was. She fought the battle with herself alone with God, came out victor, and was so cheerful, thorough, and good, that she soon

More than Conquerors

found a more congenial position. More than conqueror!

Now thanks be unto God, which always causeth us to triumph in Christ, and maketh manifest the savor of His knowledge by us in every place [leadeth us in triumph].—2 Corinthians 2:14.

The meaning of this verse is: He leadeth us in triumph, after the manner of a conqueror, acknowledged as such by all who see. We are not only enriched in ourselves by great spoils, but we have influence and leadership over others.

What are the spoils you have won in conquering, whether over sin or sorrow? Not only are you conscious of having gained the place of command instead of being led captive, but you have inward strength, calm confidence, knowledge of Christ, enlarged views of God, gentleness, love, meekness, brotherly kindness, enrichment of the whole being. Your trials are bread for you. Jesus was not only victor, but He led captivity captive and gave gifts unto men. "As I have overcome, so will I grant to him that overcometh."

"It will sometimes be discovered that in actual life there are two kinds of heroes —heroes for the visible, and heroes for the invisible; they that see their mark as a flag hung out to be taken upon some turret or battlement, and they that see it nowhere save in the grand ideal of the inward life: *extempore* heroes fighting out a victory definitely seen in something near at hand; and the life-long, century-long, heroes that are instigated by no ephemeral crown or mere ephemeral passion, but have sounded the deep base-work of God's principle, and have dared calmly to rest their all upon it, come the issue where it may or when it may or in what form God may give it. The former class are only symbols, I conceive, in the visible life, of that more heroic and truly divine greatness in the other, which is never offered to the eyes in forms of palpable achievement."

How perfectly in accord with the Word is the thought in this quotation! God's heroes are not all written in history. Some of them are unknown even to their every-day companions. To those of us who live in "the daily round, the common task," and yet have aspirations outreaching our surroundings, how inspiriting it is to know that however we may seem to others, or to ourselves, God may count us in the ranks of His most courageous victors! There are sweet surprises awaiting many a humble soul fighting against great odds in the battle of a seemingly commonplace life. It has never entered the thought of that gentle woman whom we met the other day, that her name stands among the first in the list of God's heroines. She rarely meets anyone outside of her family circle, except when she greets her neighbors at the Sunday morning service. She is never seen in social gatherings nor in conventions where other women have their souls stirred to do great and heroic things for the cause of truth, because she never has the opportunity. Her hands are filled with ordinary tasks. An invalid in the household demands her thought and care; and that which tests her heroism most is the agony of knowing that he who ought to be her strength and help does her cruel wrong by his selfish, sinful life. Yet you would not suspect her sorrow in the calm, bright face; you hear no word of complaint from the guarded lips. That woman is not simply a meek sufferer—she is a joyful victor; for she has heard with spiritual ear the triumphant word of the Spirit, "To him that overcometh will I give to eat of the hidden manna."

God's heroes are often entirely unrecognized, even by those who dwell in the same household. One sees nothing in their outward life to call for the exercise of heroic qualities; it would seem there is scarcely enough of trial to develop a good degree of spiritual strength. But there are mental struggles and self-conquests, known to Him who discerns the secrets of the heart, which may place one high in the ranks of His nobility.

The patient endurance of unjust judgments, the silent committal of misunderstandings to Him who judgeth righteously, the setting aside of personal preference for others when it is least appreciated—all these mark the heroic soul, and place it among the shining ones who " overcome "; for it is written, " Better is he who ruleth his spirit than he that taketh a city." To see one mark in the " grand ideal of the inward life," and to reach it by successive victories over self and sin in the most ordinary affairs of every day, may prove better for us in the end than to hold a conspicuous place even in the greatest and best causes.

In the final contest, as pictured by the Revealer, when the hosts of evil make war with the Lamb, those that are with Him, going forth conquering and to conquer, are " called and chosen and faithful," and doubtless many whose days have been spent in quiet country farmhouses, or in unobtrusive ways of life elsewhere, will occupy high places of honor in that victorious company.

THE MOUNTAINEER'S PRAYER.

Gird me with the strength of Thy steadfast hills,
   The speed of Thy streams give me ;
In the spirit that calms or the life that thrills,
   I would stand or run for Thee.

Let me be Thy voice, or Thy silent power,
   As the cataract or the peak,—
An eternal thought in my earthly hour,
   Of the living God to speak.

Clothe me in the rose-tints of Thy skies
   Upon morning summits laid,
Robe me in the purple and gold that flies
   Through Thy shuttles of light and shade.

Let me rise and rejoice in Thy smile aright
   As mountains and forests do ;
Let me welcome Thy twilight and Thy night,
   And wait for Thy dawn anew.

Give me of the brook's song joyously sung
   Under clank of icy chain,
Give me of the patience that hides among
   Thy hilltops in mist and rain.

Lift me up from the clod, let me breathe Thy breath ;
   Thy beauty and strength give me ;
Let me lose both the name and the meaning of death
   In the life that I live with Thee !
                           LUCY LARCOM.

June

What Do Ye More than Others?

And if ye salute your brethren only, what do ye more than others?—Matthew 5 : 47.

IT is the glory of our blessed religion, the grace and truth which came by Jesus Christ, that it proposes to do more for humanity than any other religion or system of morals has ever proposed, and it consequently expects more of its followers. Not that it lays heavy burdens upon us, under which we must faint and despair ; no — other religions do that, while they promise so little in return for the effort. But our blessed faith holds out to us inspiring possibilities, a height of character, a plane of living, a " glory of

More than Others

helpfulness," a power to be and do for others, which shows that it never was born of human thought, but carries with it the impress of divinity.

What, followers of Jesus, what do ye more than others? The question is a challenge; it is an inspiration too. It puts a Christian on his honor. It shows that we have " a high calling of God in Christ Jesus "— something better than the best outside of the life hid with Christ in God.

Except your righteousness shall exceed the righteousness of the scribes and Pharisees, ye shall in no wise enter the kingdom of heaven.—Matthew 5:20.

Not that you shall not get to heaven, but you shall fall far short of the high honor and blessedness of participating in the purpose, spirit, and rewards of the kingdom here.

What do ye more than others? If you live according to standards of the world, if you take its maxims as your guide, you do no more. Our faith is eminently practical. How do we compare in spirit and in outward life with those nearest us, in our own homes, who are not Christians? It is said, a traveler once visiting the lighthouse at Calais said to the keeper: " But what if one of your lights should go out at night!" " Never — impossible!" he cried. " Sir, yonder are ships sailing to all parts of the world. If to-night one of my burners were out, in six months I should hear from America, or India, saying that on such a night the lights at Calais lighthouse gave no warning, and some vessel had been wrecked. Ah, sir, sometimes I feel, when I look upon my lights, as if the eyes of the whole world were fixed upon me. Go out! Burn dim! Never! Impossible!"

Ye are the salt of the earth: but if the salt have lost his savor, wherewith shall it be salted? it is thenceforth good for nothing, but to be cast out, and to be trodden under foot of men. Ye are the light of the world. A city that is set on a hill cannot be hid. Neither do men light a candle, and put it under a bushel, but on a candlestick; and it giveth light unto all that are in the house. Let your light so shine before men, that they may see your good works, and glorify your Father which is in heaven.—Matt. 5 : 13-16.

In the Sermon on the Mount, Jesus gives us a philosophy of life very unlike the teachings of the world. He tells us how to live gloriously, victoriously; possessors of the kingdom. Nor has He given us theories, but practical principles which, by the power He Himself will put within us, we may show forth in our daily conduct. Nor has He given them to us for our profit alone: what we have learned of Him we are to use for the help of others. We, Christians, who have been taught of the Spirit through the Word, are to be the salt of the earth, the light of the world. That ye may be blameless and harmless, the sons of God, without rebuke, in the midst of a crooked and perverse nation, among whom ye shine as lights in the world.—Phil. 2 : 15. For ye were sometimes darkness, but now are ye light in the Lord : walk as children of light.—Ephesians 5 : 8.

I wish we might get a new view of the responsibility, the dignity, the blessedness of being a Christian ; not for our own sakes so much as for the sake of others. It is a great joy to be of use. It was for the joy set before Him of saving this world that the Lord Jesus endured the cross, despising the shame. Did you ever feel a richer thrill in your heart than when someone said to you : " You have helped me so much—your words have been a blessing to me ; your life, as I have watched it, has been an inspiration and strength to me"? There is no cup so sweet to the taste as this—the joy of doing good. It seems as if we might preface these words with the "blessed" of each beatitude. "Blessed are ye, for ye are the salt of the earth"; "Blessed are ye, for ye are the light of the world."

But ye are a chosen generation, a royal priesthood, a holy nation, a peculiar people; that ye should shew forth the praises of Him who hath called you out of darkness into His marvelous light.— 1 Peter 2:9.

What is the standard of conduct for Christians? One would think, judging from the sight of the eyes, that the answer to this question is, "Prevailing opinion." If the drift is in a certain direction, conviction and conscience seem to float with the tide. A few years ago, in the Church the theater-goers were conspicuous, and felt obliged to apologize for their indulgence to their more conscientious associates. Now the tide in that direction has gained such force in many churches, happily not in all, that the question of its consistency with a true Christian life is scarcely raised, or if raised is answered to seeming satisfaction with the announcement: "Oh, everybody goes to the theater now; sentiment has changed on that subject."

We do not intend at present to discuss theater-going especially. That is only one of the many breaks in the old-time barriers between the gay world and the Christian Church. But this point of the true standard of conduct touches all questions of conscience. There seems to be in the minds of many people a varying scale by which they determine the moral weight of actions according to the personality of those who perform them. One class of Christians, they say, may allow themselves certain indulgences which their own moral sense declares improper for others. We admit this sort of judgment as regards the relative propriety of these things for the people who make no profession whatever of godly living, and for those who do make such a profession. But for such discriminations between Christians we can see no warrant in the Bible, or in sound philosophy and common-sense. Where in all the Saviour's laws of conduct did He discriminate between His followers? When He laid down the underlying principle of right living, He said to them all: "Whosoever will be my disciple, let him deny himself, and take up his cross daily, and follow me."

Where in any of the apostles' teachings do we learn that a part of the Christian Church is under obligation to "do all to the glory of God," and the rest may glorify and indulge self "according to the course of this world"? Why should the members of a church be shocked at the thought of their minister attending the various performances in which they themselves find so much pleasure? They do feel so. They would honestly feel pained to remember on Sunday morning, as they listen to his spiritual teaching, that they had seen him during the week under such circumstances. Why? Let us look the question fairly in the face, and see if there is any warrant for making these distinctions. If the thing is right for any Christian, we believe it is right for all; if wrong for any, it is wrong for all. We have beclouded conscience and "caused our weak brother to offend" too long by such false standards of conduct. The only safe and really honest thing for every professed follower of Jesus to do is to bring all questionable indulgences, all that have the possible savor of "the things that are in the world, the lust of the flesh, the lust of the eyes, and the pride of life," to the Bible standard of Christian living, and decide accordingly.

This standard is plain enough. Everything that helps to build up a true, noble, beautiful character; all that works harmoniously with God's plan for our personal perfection or the extending of His kingdom among men, is right for a Christian to enter into and enjoy. All that does not minister to these things is manifestly out of the range of genuine Christian living. There is but one standard for all, and that standard is not popular opinion, but loyalty to Christ and to the extension of His kingdom in the hearts of men. Let the reason for our action in every case be the only honorable reason for a Christian, "*for this is right.*"

What do ye more than others as an antiseptic quality in society? If the salt has lost its savor, it is henceforth good for nothing. Thrown out upon the roadways, it kills all vegetable life. This illustrates not only the uselessness but the harmfulness of Christians who have no positive convictions, who are so like the world in manner and spirit that no one can discover any influence coming from them for good. Salt must be in the food, and in the substance in which we would arrest decay: so Christians must be in the world, but not lose their antiseptic quality. I pray not that Thou shouldest take them out of the world, but that Thou shouldest keep them from the evil.—John 17: 15.

"And both Jesus was called, and His disciples, to the marriage." We have here one of several glimpses given us of the social life of the Lord Jesus, when for the time He was our fellow-citizen upon earth. He was invited to a marriage reception, and accepted the invitation; and in other instances we find Him dining with a large company. His example, then, settles for us, as Christians, the question, "Is it right for me to enjoy social festivities?" There was nothing ascetic in the life or teachings of Jesus.

More than Others

He kept Himself in sympathy with humanity; human joys, human relationships, as well as human sorrows, found in Him the responsive heart of a brother. Wherever He went, whether to the marriage or the burial, His mission was by His presence, His words, and His acts to brighten and cheer. At every social gathering in which we find Him, it is evident that there " He went about doing good," just the same as when He fed and healed the people by the wayside.

His example, in respect to accepting invitations and enjoying social life, most of us are very ready to follow; but how about our mission and our deportment at an evening reception ? As a rule, do we follow the Master there in going about doing good ? " What! would you have me talk only on religion, and urge everybody I meet to attend to their Christian duties, as if I were exhorting in a prayer-meeting ?" Oh no, surely not, unless such a thing should come about most naturally and easily in the course of conversation.

But surely the " speech " of a Christian should be " always with grace, seasoned with salt "; that is, it ought to have something in it that is different from the vapid, senseless, and too often unwholesome chatter of " society."

Then, too, if one is in the spirit of it, there are abundant opportunities to say really helpful things here and there, which may even do more good than an out-and-out exhortation at a prayer-meeting. There are silent ways of doing good also. A marked silence in the face of wrong is often more eloquent than speech, and even the *eyes* of a Christian may be very effective in their expression of disapproval.

Certainly no Christian woman is following her Master in doing good when she conforms to certain modes of dress now prevalent in society. We know this is delicate ground upon which we tread. But it is too serious a matter for Christians to ignore. Mothers have a great responsibility just at this point, both as to their own example and in the training of their daughters. The world has not yet so far regained its Eden purity as that they have no need to heed the exhortation to "adorn themselves in modest apparel, with shamefacedness and sobriety," in a manner "which becometh women professing godliness."

There is one law for us all by which we may be in the world and yet "kept from the evil." It is this: "Whatsoever ye do in word or deed, do all in the name of the Lord Jesus." Following this rule, it may be said of every occasion, not that we are there without Him, but that "both Jesus and His disciples are called," and are together at the feast.

There is a silent power which we exert whether conscious of it or not, as flowers breathe their fragrance. A friend said of another whose character was pure and gentle, "An hour with that man does me more good than a sermon." Of Jesus it is said, virtue went out from Him. So it must be with His followers who are partakers of the divine nature.

What do ye more than others in the spirit of forgiveness?

I say unto you, Love your enemies, bless them that curse you, do good to them that hate you, and pray for them which despitefully use you, and persecute you.—Matthew 5:44.

Let all bitterness, and wrath, and anger, and clamor, and evil speaking, be put away from you, with all malice. And be ye kind to one another, tender-hearted, forgiving one another, even as God for Christ's sake hath forgiven you.—Ephesians 4:31, 32.

Be ye therefore followers of God, as dear children.—Ephesians 5:1.

That ye may be the children of your Father which is in heaven: for He maketh His sun to rise on the evil and on the good, and sendeth rain on the just and on the unjust.—Matthew 5:45.

Therefore if thine enemy hunger, feed him; if he thirst, give him drink: for in so doing thou shalt heap coals of fire on his head. Be not overcome of evil, but overcome evil with good.—Romans 12: 20, 21.

What do you more in self-control? For this is thankworthy, if a man for conscience toward God endure grief, suffering wrongfully. For what glory is it, if, when ye be buffeted for your faults, ye shall take it patiently? but if, when ye do well, and suffer for it, ye take it patiently, this is acceptable with God.— 1 Peter 2: 19, 20.

And what are you as a Christian doing more than others in the grace of cheerfulness? Your face should be " like the

morning while the days are going by."
A Christian has no right to go about the
world with a gloomy face. How it cheers
you to meet a friend who gives you a
bright salutation as you are going down
the street! We can scarcely measure the
influence of our face and manner upon
those with whom we associate, especially
upon little children.

There was a poor tired woman with
whom things had gone wrong all day.
She felt her lot was hard, to be baking
and scrubbing while her neighbor just
over the fence was lying at ease in her
hammock out under the trees and singing,

"Oh, nobody knows the trouble I see."

Presently a door was opened softly, and
her little daughter picked her way with
prudent steps where the floor had not been
wet, and climbed to a safe perch on the
table. The mother mopped away, hoping
she need not speak to her. "If I open

my mouth I shall say something cross," she thought, and kept her lips shut tightly. The little one watched her for a short time, bending her sunny head this way and that to study the downcast countenance, and finally she spoke. " Mamma," said she, " I have hardly ever seen you without a smile on your face." The mother turned away for a moment's rapid thought. Was it indeed true that she had made such an impression on that dear child's heart; and should she spoil it now? Should she not rather set herself thenceforth to keep a smiling face through all life's petty trials? How sweet to be remembered thus by all the children, and her husband too, for pleasant looks and ways! " One time when you looked sorry was when I was sick, and the other time was now," resumed the serious little voice; and the child leaned her cheek upon her hand and sighed. The mop-handle dropped suddenly upon the floor, and two bare arms forgot their aches and pains and clasped the darling in a fond embrace. " Sing to me, Alice. Sing ' Nobody knows the comfort I have,' while I finish this patch of dirty floor. There's one good thing about a little tucked-up kitchen, it doesn't take long to scrub it!"

A mother once said: " I find I cannot keep my house and temper both in perfect order at the same time, so I do the best I can about my house, and care more about my temper." That was decidedly the proper thing for a Christian to do.

What do ye more in the spirit of charity? If anyone should be lenient to the faults and failings of others, surely it should be the Christian who has had much forgiven. And above all things have fervent charity among yourselves: for charity shall cover the multitude of sins.—1 Peter 4: 8.

"Dear moss," said the old thatch, " I am so old, so patched, so ragged, really I am quite unsightly. I wish you would come and cheer me up a little. You will hide my infirmities, and through your love and sympathy no finger of contempt or dislike will be pointed at me." "I will come," said the moss, and it crept up and over, and in and out, until every flaw was hidden and all was smooth and fair. Presently the sun shone out, and the old thatch looked glorious in its rays. "How beautiful the thatch looks!" cried one and another. "Ah!" said the old thatch, "rather let them say, 'How beautiful is the love of the moss!' which spreads itself and covers all my faults and keeps the knowledge of them to herself, by her own grace casting over me a beautiful carpet of freshness and verdure."

What do ye more than others in taking an interest in humanity? " If you salute your brethren only, what do ye more than others?" It has been said truly, if one is not stirred in soul and stirred to do something to help in view of the state of things around him, he had better inquire seriously into his own condition of heart. The impulse of the Christian should be that of helpfulness under all circumstances. A young lady, while on her way home from Sunday morning service, came unexpectedly upon an old schoolmate in so thoroughly an intoxicated condition that she could scarcely walk. She had been seen by others, but they, like the priest and the Levite, had passed her by unheeded. The lady, greatly shocked, recognized her sad condition, and without a moment's hesitation, determined to take her home to her widowed mother. This could be done only by supporting her by her arm and half carrying her; in order to render this service, she must traverse the principal street of the town, and expose herself to the curious glances, and perhaps the uncharitable judgment, of those who might see her in so strange a position. Yet the help was resolutely rendered, and the erring daughter was returned to her anxious mother.

St. Paul says: " Bear ye one another's burdens." It is a trite saying, but true, that men will not read their Bibles, but they will read you. We are living epistles of Christ, known and read of all men. In our work, in our home, many eyes are upon us. How will we meet this temptation, with what grace will we bear this sorrow, with what patience will we endure this trial, with what fidelity will we meet this duty ? Jesus stands by every counter, by every typewriter, by every mother, daughter, sister, and " with those eyes so pure and tender," waits to see if we reflect His light steadily and clearly. Does it go out, burn dim ? Ah! then you hide from somebody who needs Him so much, the world's Saviour.

They are asking, " Can any good thing come out of Nazareth ? " Are we answering, " Come and see " ? They are asking, " Is there a balm in Gilead, is there a Physician there ? " Are we answering, " Yes, for I have proved His power " ? Over this storm-swept sea of human sin and sorrow, many a brave seaman is stemming frightful tides. Frost-bitten, almost frozen to the heart, in the midst of the struggle they are looking out for the harbor lights. They believe there is a harbor, but the rocks are on every side, and the tempest is hard to combat. Oh, what if, as they are seeking to enter the harbor of safety in the world's Redeemer, your light or mine should lead them astray, or should burn so dimly as to make them less sure that there is a harbor to be found ?

EVENING.

Slowly shadows creep over the lea,
Deep'ning and lengthening silently,
Stretching away toward the setting sun—
Life's busy, bright day is almost done.

In the early morn we started forth,
When dew was fresh on the tender earth,
And the happy songs on sweet air borne
With an inspiration filled the morn.

Not alone were we in those bright hours,
For many and true the friendships ours;
And love grew ever more close and sweet,
As we trod life's way with eager feet.

But one by one they have stepped aside
Into a bark on a mystic tide;
We strain our vision, but catch no gleam
Of fading forms far over the stream.

Then we closer clasp the hands that stay,
And thoughtfully tread life's changing way;
And we watch the evening mists that rise
From landscape gray to the glowing skies.

As the night steals on I may not know
What loving hand from my clasp shall go;
When the fading light of day is done
I may stand by the river's brink alone.

But beyond the twilight, day will rise;
Eternal glory brightens the skies;
A new, glad morning will be begun,
Never to close with a setting sun.

E. J. K.

July

My Care

Casting all your care upon Him, for He careth for you.—*1 Peter 5 : 7.*

MY weight of care—what shall I do with it? I am very tired, and not very strong, and the weight is heavy, no matter how much I try to make light of it. The years, from which I hoped so much, have come and gone, and when I thought to have my care greatly lessened I find it increased. If I think to share it with another, and thus lighten it for myself, I see that it is a grievous mistake. I only add to my friend's burden, and get no relief from my own. I suppose I must carry, it then, to the end, and grow old and heavy-hearted, with the luster gone

My Care

from my eyes, and the song silent in my heart.

But let me consider. Is this the only disposal that can be made of my care? When I look at it squarely, with all its attendant circumstances, I do not see any probability of its removal; I think it has somehow grown into the fiber, so that the earthly life and the care will live and die together. The first thing, then, that I can do is to accept this fact courageously; for a mind made up to take things as they are, when they cannot be altered, is itself a comfort and strength.

I have learned, in whatsoever state I am, therewith to be content. I can do all things through Christ which strengtheneth me.—Phil. 4: 11, 13.

I can also look over my burden carefully, and see if there is anything in it which does not belong there. For instance, all this restless anxiety and questioning about the future regarding things temporal or eternal ought not to add its weight to my care, for the Lord has plainly told me that I cannot control those things any more than I can add one cubit to my stature, and that He does keep His own hand upon them to manage all for my good.

And which of you by taking thought can add one cubit unto his stature? If ye then be not able to do that which is least, why take ye thought for the rest? And your Father knoweth that ye have need of these things.—Luke 12: 24, 25, 30.

So, burdensome anxiety about these things is not legitimate care for a Christian. There is, too, an undue solicitude about His work which surely it does not please Him to have me carry. He asks me only to be obedient and faithful and leave results with Him, and it seems like an impertinence really for me to be anxious, as if God did not understand and could not manage the affairs of His own kingdom.

So then neither is he that planteth anything, neither he that watereth; but God that giveth the increase.—1 Cor. 3:7.

Having sorted it all over, however, and left out everything which ought not to rest with any discomfort upon me, there is still left a *real care* which appears to belong to my life. Well, then, it must be mine for my good. My Father never gave me a stone when I sincerely asked Him for bread. This care, therefore, is not to be a burden, crushing out my truest life, but as bread to nourish and strengthen it. How ? By bringing me into fellowship with Jesus. This unavoidable sorrow and disappointment teaches me the fellowship of His sufferings; it reveals to me His compassion; it shows me how out of weakness He can make me strong; it brings me so near to

Him while I talk with Him about it that I feel as if the bitterness itself had almost turned to sweetness, because through it I have learned to know Him more perfectly. Most gladly, therefore, will I rather glory in my necessary care, but the *weight* of it I will cast upon Him, for I know surely that He careth for me.

Wherein ye greatly rejoice, though now for a season if need be ye are in heaviness through manifold temptations [trials]. That the trial of your faith, being much more precious than of gold that perisheth, though it be tried with fire, might be found unto praise and honor and glory at the appearing of Jesus Christ.—1 Peter 1:6, 7.

So, whatever my care, it need never be a burden. Cast thy burden upon the Lord, and He shall sustain thee: He shall never suffer the righteous to be moved.—Psalm 55:22. The Lord also will be a refuge for the oppressed, a refuge in times of trouble. And they that know Thy Name will put their trust in Thee: for Thou, Lord, hast not forsaken them that seek Thee.—Psalm 9:9.

It was a day which promised to be full of hardships; a day that would ruffle the spirit like wind-swept water. Opening her *Daily Light upon the Daily Path*, one read, "Thou wilt keep him in perfect peace whose mind is stayed on Thee, because he trusteth in Thee."

"Can it be possible? Perfect peace? He says so; I will test Him. My mind, so far as I am able to control it, shall be stayed upon Him. I will, as far as I can in my weakness, trust Him. Heavenly Father, help me faithfully upon my part to test the faithfulness of Thy word this day." Nothing was changed in the circumstances of each hour, except that things were a little more trying than had been anticipated. But whenever her heart was about to give way she would look up and say: "Thou hast said it, Lord. Thou wilt keep in perfect peace the mind that is stayed on Thee. How can it be stayed on Thee when things are so distracting and so hard? But Thou wilt keep! I give my mind into Thy keeping"; and, true to His word, He whispered peace in her heart so blessedly that when the day was over she said: "It has indeed been a hard day, but oh, so sweet! I never should have known the preciousness of the promise if the need of testing it had not been so sorely pressed upon me."

Thus writes another who has set to her seal that God is true: "It is a transforming, almost a glorifying, thing to gladly welcome, yes, pray for, all of God's will when the 'all' evidently includes much pain and limitation. I do not understand how people can endure to live in this world without God and without hope. He is such a comfort and assurance to me that if I had not already committed all to Him I would do so before finishing this letter. It took me a long time to get everything committed. There were a few reserves I wished to make. Chiefly, I did not wish to become dependent upon others, and I feared a chronic illness toward which I thought I might be tending. Finally, the good Father brought me where I was willing to become a street beggar and helpless if He saw it best. That gave me rest. It is so evident that we know nothing. Why should we rack our poor brains over problems we can never solve and conditions we can never change? Better to refer the whole matter to our Father, and simply obey and trust Him."

It is interesting to remember that it is Peter who writes these words: " Casting all your care upon Him, for He careth for you,"— Peter, who had so many marked experiences of the care of Jesus.

It seems as if he says to each one of us personally:

"Does life press heavily? Is there something which gives you anxiety? Let me tell you what to do. I can tell you, not only because I have been taught of the Spirit, but also because I have learned by experience. There was a time in my life when I did not know Jesus, the Saviour, the burden-bearer, the 'consolation of Israel.' I was a fisherman. I spent my life in daily toil—real hard work, earning just enough to keep myself and my family supplied with the necessities of life. There was nothing very inspiring or uplifting in the monotony of my toil. One day, as I was casting my net into the sea,—just doing my ordinary work,—Jesus passed by, and said to me and to my brother Andrew, who was with me, 'Follow me, and I will make you fishers of men.' I did not fully understand His call, but I knew it meant something better than working solely and only for my daily bread; so I followed Him. Oh, what a day was that for me! It was the beginning of a new life. I began that day to learn what it meant that Jesus, the Redeemer of men, the Lord of heaven and earth, cared for me. I was still a fisherman. Many days after that I worked, and was weary; but even my work seemed different, because I knew my mission; while I toiled for necessary temporal supplies it was linked with higher things. He had said I should be a fisher of men; He would use me in blessing others. I saw that He cared too much for me to let me be *only* a fisherman, with no thought or purpose higher than my daily bread. Oh, what a day for every toiler when Jesus comes into the life!"

And whatsoever ye do, do it heartily as to the Lord and not unto men; knowing that of the Lord ye shall receive the reward of the inheritance: for ye serve the Lord Christ.—Col. 3: 23, 24.

With good will doing service, as to the Lord, and not to men : knowing that whatsoever good thing any man doeth, the same shall he receive of the Lord, whether he be bond or free. — Eph. 6: 7, 8.

"At another time, after He had risen from the grave, He showed His care for me by telling me where to cast my net; so I know also that He can and does direct me in my work, and teach me how to be successful in it. He cared for me when my family was in trouble through illness. My wife's mother was sick with a fever. We told Jesus, and He came immediately and cured her. Once I was about to sink in the water, because I did not trust Him perfectly, but even then He cared for me, and put out His hand and caught me. After the Lord had ascended to heaven, I was shut up in prison because I had borne my testimony for Him among the Jews who crucified Him, and in answer to the prayers of my friends He sent His angel to open the prison doors."

For He hath said, I will never leave thee nor forsake thee.—Heb. 13:5.

And behold I am with thee, and will keep thee in all places whither thou goest. —Gen. 28:15.

And the Lord, He it is that doth go before thee; He will be with thee, He will not fail thee, neither forsake thee: fear not, neither be dismayed.—Deut. 31:8.

Be strong and of a good courage, *and do it:* fear not, nor be dismayed: for the Lord God, even my God, will be with Thee; He will not fail thee, nor forsake thee, until thou hast finished all the work for the service of the house of the Lord. —1 Chron. 28:20.

" But oh, best of all, I know that He cares for me even when I have not been true to Him. I denied Him before His enemies. I even said I had never known Him. O those eyes when He turned and looked upon me! I can never forget; it broke my heart. Such pitying, forgiving, entreating love! And after His resurrection He sent Mary to tell me, the faithless one, that He had risen. Now I am an old man; believe me when I tell you from a life of long experience that you may cast all your care upon Him, for He careth for you."

With Peter's experience confirmed by the word of the Lord, we will

> " Drop our burden at His feet
> And bear a song away."

My Care

HE CARETH FOR ME.

Casting all your care upon Him, for He careth for you.—1 Peter 5.: 7.

What can it mean? Is it aught to Him
That the nights are long and the days are dim;
Can He be touched by the griefs I bear,
Which sadden the heart and whiten the hair?
Around His throne are eternal calms,
And strong, glad music of happy psalms,
And bliss unruffled by any strife—
How can He care for my poor life?

And yet I want Him to care for me,
While I live in this world where the sorrows be.
When the lights die down on the path I take;
When strength is feeble, and friends forsake;
When love and music, that once did bless,
Have left me to silence and loneliness;
And life-song changes to sobbing prayers—
Then my heart cries out for a God who cares.

When shadows hang o'er me the whole day long,
And my spirit is bowed with shame and wrong;
When I am not good, and the deeper shade
Of conscious sin makes my heart afraid;
And the busy world has too much to do
To stay in its course to help me through;

156 Spirit and Life

And I long for a Saviour—can it be
That the God of the universe cares for me?

Oh, wonderful story of deathless love!
Each child is dear to that heart above;
He fights for me when I cannot fight;
He comforts me in the gloom of night;
He lifts the burden, for He is strong;
He stills the sigh and wakens the song.
The sorrow that bowed me down He bears,
And loves and pardons, because He cares.

Let all who are sad take heart again—
We are not alone in our hours of pain;
Our Father stoops from His throne above
To soothe and quiet us with His love.
He leaves us not when the storm is high,
And we have safety, for He is nigh.
Can it be trouble which He doth share?
Oh, rest in peace, for the Lord *does* care.

Selected.

August

A Light in a Dark Place

We have also a more sure word of prophecy; whereunto ye do well that ye take heed, as unto a light that shineth in a dark place.
—2 Peter 1 : 19.

A FRIEND of mine, not long since visiting the Mammoth Cave in Kentucky, vividly describes the effect of a lamp shining in a dark place, and the utter helplessness of travelers in the darkness without that light. The guide went before with a lamp, by which they not only walked quite safely, but also saw the wonderful formations upon the walls of the cave, and its surprises in new openings constantly rising before them. Suddenly the man with the lamp disappeared. Everyone stood still, afraid to take a step in the darkness and uncertainty. "What does it mean? Where has he gone? How shall we ever find our way either backward or forward?" They called; no answer. For a few moments, which seemed long to the bewildered travelers, they waited in suspense. Suddenly the cheerful voice of the guide called out, "See!" and as his light flashed before them, the most beautiful of all the places in the cave was revealed. He had only stepped into a recess where his light was hidden, that he might give them this pleasant surprise.

What the great cave in its bewildering darkness was to my friend, this world is to human souls without the light of this precious word. I would like to talk with you, simply, earnestly, with the help of the Spirit, about your Bible—the book without which you and I are in helpless darkness whether we know it or not; the book which, like the lamp of the guide,

A Light in a Dark Place

will not only conduct us safely through the difficult and dangerous places, but will also reveal to us the thoughts of God, beautiful and precious, like the sparkling stalactites hanging from the roof of the cave.

There are fishes in the streams in this cave having "eyes which see not." The place for eyes is there as in other fish, but they have lived so long in the dark, this organ has become utterly useless. It may be so with us. We have the ability given us to read and understand this book, but by long neglect we lose our power to comprehend it. It is a great loss. I earnestly pray that your Bible may be to you truly a lamp unto your feet, and that you will love it so that you will say as the prophet:

Thy words were found, and I did eat them; and Thy word was unto me the joy and rejoicing of mine heart.—Jeremiah 15:16.

First of all, do you realize that your Bible is the word of God? Is it not reasonable to believe that the God who made us and sent us into this world, would in some way make known to us His will; that He would give us some directions how to live; how to get out of any difficulties, and what to look forward to in that future, the prophecy of which is in every human consciousness? There never was a time when this blessed book was the subject of so much intelligent scrutiny as now. Intellect and learning have turned their electric light upon it, and some have been so dazzled by this light that they have lost sight of the steady flame of the Lamp itself. But it burns without a flicker of doubt in the midst of high winds of criticism and gales of unbelief, for all who take it as the sure word of prophecy, which came not by the will of man, but by holy men who spoke as they were moved by the Holy Ghost.

A Light in a Dark Place

The entrance of the Word is giving light in every part of the world to-day, and we have more help for its study than ever before. But do not let us take our instruction too much through human channels. There is no preaching, no Bible readings, that can take the place of a personal acquaintance with one's own Bible. No one can be a strong, growing Christian who does not "feed upon" the sincere milk, as well as the strong meat, of the Word. Let us take it without human comment, as it is given to us by the Great Teacher, the Holy Spirit. It is beyond the reach of highest intellect to understand, but even a child by reading it is made wise unto salvation. Let it speak for itself in its own inspired words.

For this cause also thank we God without ceasing, because, when ye received the word of God which ye heard of us, ye received it not as the word of men, but, as it is in truth, the word of God, which effectually worketh also in you that believe.—1 Thessalonians 2:13. [That is to say, it shows its energy in its practical effects on you that believe.]

For I am not ashamed of the gospel of Christ: for it is the power of God unto salvation to everyone that believeth; to the Jew first, and also to the Greek.—Romans 1:16.

Ye shall not add unto the word which I command you, neither shall ye diminish aught from it, that ye may keep the commandments of the Lord your God which I command you.—Deuteronomy 4:2.

For what is it given us?

But continue thou in the things which thou hast learned and hast been assured of, knowing of whom thou hast learned them; and that from a child thou hast known the holy Scriptures, which are able to make thee wise unto salvation through faith which is in Christ Jesus. All Scripture is given by inspiration of God, and is

A Light in a Dark Place

profitable for doctrine, for reproof, for correction, for instruction in righteousness. That the man of God may be perfect, thoroughly furnished unto all good works.—2 Tim. 3: 14-17.

For doctrine, such a standard is needed especially now.

Now the Spirit speaketh expressly, that in the latter times some shall depart from the faith, giving heed to seducing spirits, and doctrines of devils.—1 Timothy 4: 1.

I charge thee therefore before God, and the Lord Jesus Christ, who shall judge the quick and the dead at His appearing and His kingdom; preach the word; be instant in season, out of season; reprove, rebuke, exhort with all longsuffering and doctrine. For the time will come when they will not endure sound doctrine; but after their own lusts shall they heap to themselves teachers, having itching ears; and they shall turn away their ears from the truth, and shall be turned unto fables.

But watch thou in all things, endure afflictions, do the work of an evangelist, make full proof of thy ministry.—2 Timothy 4: 1–5.

If any man teach otherwise, and consent not to wholesome words, even the words of our Lord Jesus Christ, and to the doctrine which is according to godliness; he is proud, knowing nothing, but doting about questions and strifes of words, whereof cometh envy, strife, railings, evil surmisings.—1 Timothy 6: 3, 4.

The wise men are ashamed, they are dismayed and taken: lo, they have rejected the word of the Lord; and what wisdom is in them?—Jeremiah 8: 9.

The wisdom of what? Who shall answer?

To the law and to the testimony: if they speak not according to this word, it is because there is no light in them.—Isaiah 8: 20.

Holding fast the faithful word as he

hath been taught, that he may be able by sound doctrine both to exhort and to convince the gainsayers.—Titus 1:9.

For reproof also; telling a fault, convincing and convicting of sin.

The law of the Lord is perfect, converting the soul: the testimony of the Lord is sure, making wise the simple. The statutes of the Lord are right, rejoicing the heart: the commandment of the Lord is pure, enlightening the eyes. The fear of the Lord is clean, enduring forever: the judgments of the Lord are true and righteous altogether. More to be desired are they than gold, yea, than much fine gold: sweeter also than honey and the honeycomb. Moreover by them is Thy servant warned: and in keeping of them there is great reward.—Psalm 19:7-11.

By the law is the knowledge of sin.—Romans 3:20.

Was then that which is good made death unto me? God forbid. But sin, that it might appear sin, working death in me by that which is good; that sin by the commandment might become exceeding sinful.—Romans 7 : 13.

Is not my word like as a fire ? saith the Lord; and like a hammer that breaketh the rock in pieces ?—Jeremiah 23 : 29.

For the word of God is quick, and powerful, and sharper than any two-edged sword, piercing even to the dividing asunder of soul and spirit, and of the joints and marrow, and is a discerner of the thoughts and intents of the heart.—Hebrews 4 : 12.

We are to be judged by the Word.

And if any man hear my words, and believe not, I judge him not: for I came not to judge the world, but to save the world. He that rejecteth me, and receiveth not my words, hath one that judgeth him : the word that I have spoken, the same shall judge him in the last day.—John 12 : 47, 48.

A Light in a Dark Place

It is a serious mistake, then, to measure our conduct and spirit by the standards of society. It makes little difference what men think is right; the question for us is, What does God say in His Word? It is important to know the standard by which we are to be judged at the last day.

For correction. This is the same Greek word as in Luke 13:13, where the woman bowed together with infirmity and could in no wise lift up herself, was "made straight." Nothing cures our infirmities and makes us straight like the study of the Word. David says: "I will walk at liberty, for I seek Thy precepts." The people who grow crooked through a too free conscience, or who are bent over and bowed down by a too rigid conscience, are not the people who know or love the Bible best.

It seems as if God had reserved for these days of questioning and unbelief the secrets of the buried cities of Bible times. There is nothing of more thrilling interest than the discoveries of tablets, long buried under the dust of ages, which confirm the very statements of Scripture which some scholars have questioned. The stories of Egypt, of the captivity, the deliverance, the wars with the Canaanites, and with Babylon, just as we find them recorded in the books of the Pentateuch, are confirmed by these ancient tablets. The Sabbath, that blessed institution which God gave us, "that it might be well with us, and with our children forever," would not be known if we had not learned of it in the Bible. In the latter days men and women are questioning its divine sanctity and origin. It is a device of men, they say—not the command of God. A recent tablet has been found in Babylonia, showing that the institution of the Sabbath dated far back, beyond the law of Moses, to the beginning, just as the Bible tells us, and that the day was kept by those ancient people with even what we call Pharisaic strictness, and that the meaning of its name is " A day of rest for the heart." The people who work surely should prize the book which tells of a day of rest.

It is no time now for us to doubt this sure word of prophecy. Much of it has been fulfilled; all of it will be. We live in the days of its fulfillment, and blessed are they who are found watching.

Do you say: " I do not love my Bible; I cannot feel interested in it as I know I should " ? My friend, travelers might as well say, " I do not love my guide-book; I cannot feel interested in it." But how are they going to find their way to all the delightful places without it ? Well, they never do. And that is just the reason so many Christians are staying, spiritually, in malarial places, trying various tonics and afflicted with various infirmities, when, if they would only consult the guide-book, it would direct them to green pastures, living waters, glorious hills, and glowing skies, where they would take in spiritual health and strength with every breath.

Perplexing ways are before us all; tangled thickets, foggy nights, blinding storms. Well will it be for us if we have studied our guide-book thoroughly in the light.

And let us remember the only light which is clear, and never misleads, is the light of the Holy Spirit. " He shall guide you into all the truth." Do not get bewildered by what anyone says about the Bible. Read it for yourself, and take the Holy Spirit for your teacher. The Bible was not written for "literature," although it is foremost among literary productions. It was not written for scientific teaching, although its intimations of scientific truth have probably been misunderstood largely because men have not discovered the wonders of nature as God knows them.

A Light in a Dark Place

It was not written for history, although its records of ancient nations besides that of the Hebrews are invaluable.

One purpose runs through all the book, in poetry, prophecy, history—only one; that is, salvation. From beginning to end, if we read in the light of the Spirit, we see Christ the Saviour of men. This is the mystery of the saving power of the Word. Other books appeal to the mind and the heart; this goes through the mind and the heart into the deepest being, the inner self.

The recitals of the sins of men and of nations, from which one revolts who reads them without the help of the Holy Spirit, show the steady, unchanging purpose of God to overthrow wickedness and establish righteousness. "I am the Lord, I change not," is written in every line for the encouragement of all faithful believers.

The inherent power of the Word to accomplish the purpose for which it was written — that is, salvation — was illustrated recently in the case of a Japanese gentleman on a business visit to this country. He was stopping at one of the hotels in New York, and one evening took up a book lying on the table in his room, and, being a good English scholar, he became interested in reading it. It was a copy of St. John's gospel. The story fascinated him; the pathos of the trial and crucifixion of Jesus touched him; the conversation of the Lord with Nicodemus brought conviction of the need of his own soul. He inquired at the hotel where he could find a Christian teacher, and was directed to a well-known pastor of a large church near by. Several interviews were had; the way of salvation by faith in Jesus was carefully and prayerfully explained, and before the " stranger and foreigner " left this country for Japan he became, by Christian baptism, a " fel-

A Light in a Dark Place

low-citizen with the saints and of the household of God." This is one of many similar instances constantly taking place. The Word of the Lord is tried. It is a sure foundation for our faith. We cannot afford to doubt it. To the simple, devout, spiritual soul it is "sweeter than honey in the honeycomb." Cast not away, therefore, your confidence in it, for such confidence has indeed "great recompense of reward."

A light in a dark place. Yes; that day when a shadow fell across the threshold, as the messenger came to take the dearest of all from your home, it was very dark. But you opened your Bible at the fourteenth chapter of John, and you read about Jesus going to a place, a real place, with nothing intangible or doubtful about it, and that He was coming to take His loved people to be with Him in His Father's house. And you read in Revelation about the city so holy and clean no sorrow can breathe in the air, and that there all tears are wiped from all faces. And you read that because Jesus is the resurrection and the life, your beloved who believed in Him were never touched by death; and as you read, that dark shadow melted away in sunlight.

You had to walk through places darker even than the shadow of death, and the light shone from 2 Corinthians 4:16, 17: For which cause we faint not; but though our outward man perish, yet the inward man is renewed day by day. For our light affliction, which is but for a moment, worketh for us a far more exceeding and eternal weight of glory. You were discouraged about your work, and a ray fell upon you from 1 Corinthians 15:58: Therefore, my beloved brethren, be ye steadfast, unmovable, always abounding in the work of the Lord, forasmuch as ye know that your labor is not in vain in the Lord; and from 2 Chronicles 16:9:

A Light in a Dark Place

For the eyes of the Lord run to and fro throughout the whole earth, to show Himself strong in the behalf of them whose heart is perfect toward Him.

The darkness of sin was upon your heart, and you read: Come now and let us reason together, saith the Lord: though your sins be as scarlet, they shall be as white as snow; though they be red like crimson, they shall be as wool.—Isaiah 1:18. And: If we confess our sins, He is faithful and just to forgive us our sins, and to cleanse us from all unrighteousness.—1 John 1:9.

You were ill and you saw a great light shining in 2 Corinthians 12:8-10: For this thing I besought the Lord thrice, that it might depart from me. And He said unto me, My grace is sufficient for thee: for my strength is made perfect in weakness. Most gladly therefore will I rather glory in my infirmities, that the power of Christ may rest upon me.

Therefore I take pleasure in infirmities, in reproaches, in necessities, in persecutions, in distresses for Christ's sake: for when I am weak, then am I strong.

You were in straits, and there were stars in the night when you read: But my God shall supply all your need according to His riches in glory by Christ Jesus.—Philippians 4: 19.

And God is able to make all grace abound toward you, that ye always having all sufficiency in all things may abound unto every good work.—2 Corinthians 9: 8.

And then when worst came to worst, you read: " Hope thou in God, for I shall yet praise Him who is the health of my countenance and my God," and you were sure the day was coming, for " God is light, and in Him is no darkness at all."

Never was a greater fallacy or more misleading word than this: " It makes no difference what a man believes, if he is only sincere." Did it make no difference to the woman who sincerely believed she was eating mushrooms, while she was eating toadstools? A man indorsed a note for one he sincerely believed was honest and solvent, and he had to pay the debt. You may take a train believing you are going to Boston, and it may land you in Chicago. Ye do well that ye take heed unto the *sure Word*.

Mrs. Annie Besant says: " Theosophy is a restatement of the fundamental principles of religion adapted to nineteenth-century needs. Many thoughtful persons have outgrown the old orthodox needs, and we offer them a religion founded on scientific principles." The nineteenth-century heart finds its needs met in the dear old book, the same as when centuries ago the one hundred and nineteenth psalm was written.

To accept with all the heart the promises of the Father in His Word—ah, here is a mine of wealth any jeweled prince might covet! On some misty day, when you feel poor and forsaken, open the casket wherein the Father has placed within your reach His promise-jewels. Count them over. Hold them up, and see how they sparkle and glow in the light of His face. Take up this one, and see what untold wealth it represents: " When the poor and needy seek water, and there is none, and their tongue faileth for thirst, I the Lord will hear them, I the God of Israel will not forsake them. I will open rivers in high places, and fountains in the midst of the valleys: I will make the wilderness a pool of water, and the dry land springs of water." Surely, to accept with all the heart such a promise as this, is to find joy in the valley, refreshment in the wilderness, pleasant walking even in the dry and dusty road.

There stands a great museum. You

A Light in a Dark Place

are told that it is full of treasures. You visit it; enjoy part of it; wonder at more; and turn away with little interest from much that is there. But suppose one who knows all about those treasures, and who could explain and make everything interesting to you, should take you through it, what revelations you would have; how much you would learn; how much you could tell to others! The Holy Spirit takes of the things of Christ and shows them unto us. Let our prayer be, "Open Thou mine eyes that I may behold wondrous things out of Thy law."

A SUMMER BENEDICTION.

O happy one, for whom the days
   Of summer break in wonder signs,
Whose life grows pure—tuned to the praise
   Of God's own mountain priests, the pines,—
Lay down thy chain of cares and ills
   Beneath some mighty, sun-smit crest,
And, folded by the loving hills,
   Rest in the Lord.
          Rest !

O favored spirit, who shall breathe
   The wild, white incense of the sea,
And watch time's lights and shadows wreathe,
   Yet dream of all eternity ;
Forget thine old reward or blame,
   Forget thy little goal and quest,
Wrapped by the peace that hath no name,
   Rest in the Lord.
          Rest !

O home-bound soul, whose household round
   Is broken by no holiday,
Open thy doors to scent and sound,
   Let summer meet thee on thy way ;
Gather its glory and its balm,
   Make ready for thy royal guest

A Light in a Dark Place

A shrine of sweet, perpetual calm,
   Rest in the Lord.
         Rest !

And thou, O toiler in the heat,
   Whose eyes nor birds nor blossoms cheer,
Against whose thirst and longing beat
   The blaze and burden of the year ;
For thee the cold, white stars are born,
   For thee night veils the burning west ;
From crimson eve till golden morn
   Rest in the Lord.
         Rest !
           ELLEN HAMLIN BUTLER.

September

His Jewels

And they shall be mine, saith the Lord of Hosts, in that day when I make up my jewels, and I will spare them, as a man spareth his own son that serveth him.—Malachi 3 : 17.

IT is said that Russia has the finest collection of gems in the world. The cold, hard climate and unyielding soil of Siberia is a rich field for their production. And all the precious stones found there belong to the Crown. Gathered from the rough, pebbly soil, they are taken to the Government works, cut and polished, and the choicest are selected and kept for the imperial treasury. Who would expect to gather the rarest jewels from the cold, hard north ? Who would expect to find the Lord's purest and brightest ones among the bitter experiences of this world? Yet it is there He gathers them, perhaps even more than from those lives of gladness which flow like rivers of the sunny south, for His special treasure.

And they shall be mine, saith the Lord of Hosts, in that day when I make up my jewels, and I will spare them, as a man spareth his own son that serveth him.

Special treasure, the margin reads, the sorted out. Who says, " they shall be mine "? The Lord of Hosts, our King,—He of whom it is said: Worthy is the Lamb that was slain to receive power, and riches, and wisdom, and strength, and honor, and glory, and blessing.—Revelation 5: 12.

What an honor to be called His in the presence of such a company! His special treasure, not only because purchased by Him, but His by the highest possession of love.

Of whom is it said, "they shall be mine"? Then they that feared the Lord spake often one to another: and the Lord hearkened, and heard it, and a book of remembrance was written before Him for them that feared the Lord, and that thought upon His name.—Malachi 3:16.

These are in strong contrast with the people spoken of in verses 13, 14, and 15: Your words have been stout against me, saith the Lord. Yet ye say, What have we spoken so much against Thee? Ye have said, It is vain to serve God: and what profit is it that we have kept His ordinance, and that we have walked mournfully before the Lord of Hosts? And now we call the proud happy; yea, they that work wickedness are set up; yea, they that tempt God are even delivered.

They spoke often one to another. Out of the abundance of the heart the mouth speaketh. My soul shall be satisfied—

and my mouth shall praise Thee with joyful lips.—Psalm 63:5.

The Lord hearkened and heard. There is more in this expression than merely hearing and answering. It means that He gave interested attention, "bent over to hear," and responded to what His people were saying. This is the sweet fellowship of the believer with God. It surprises us to think that He can really care about what we say or think of Him. But God is love, and expressions of affection and praise are sweet to the ear of love. Whenever we talk to one another of His goodness He hears; when any dear soul, unknown to the world, and never heard of outside of her own little circle, speaks lovingly and gratefully of Him, He bends over to listen. That which we have seen and heard declare we unto you, that ye also may have fellowship with us: and truly our fellowship is with the Father, and with His Son, Jesus Christ.—1 John 1:3.

A book of remembrance was written before Him. Does He care so much, that He keeps in a book what we say? Oh, I wonder if I ever said anything of my God, loving and tender and grateful enough for Him to remember! I hope He will forget the distrustful and unthankful things I have said. I pray that He may cast them behind His back, with my sins forever.

There is one writing of remembrance that I am glad to think of: Behold, I have graven thee upon the palms of my hands.—Isaiah 49: 16.

Those pierced hands—when I think of them I am no longer afraid of God's book of remembrance of me, for He hath remembered His covenant forever.—Psalm 105: 8.

The book was kept for them that thought upon His name. It means more than thinking of Him. The word signifies that they were careful for the honor of

His Jewels

His name. As His friends, they would bring no reproach upon it. His word, His cause, were dear to them; the interests of His kingdom were first in their thoughts. These are they which follow the Lamb, whithersoever He goeth.—Revelation 14:4. They are the sealed ones of whom we read in Revelation, seventh chapter, and in Ephesians 4:30: Grieve not the Holy Spirit of God, whereby ye are sealed unto the day of redemption.

Whosoever therefore shall confess me before men, him will I confess also before my Father which is in heaven.—Matthew 10:32.

Whosoever therefore shall be ashamed of me and my words, in this adulterous and sinful generation, of him also shall the Son of man be ashamed, when He cometh in the glory of His Father with the holy angels.—Mark 8:38.

These, then, are His jewels, who, out of

loving hearts, talked of Him, thought of Him, and honored His name.

Now therefore, if ye will obey my voice indeed, and keep My covenant, then ye shall be a peculiar treasure unto me above all people: for all the earth is mine. And ye shall be unto me a kingdom of priests, and a holy nation. These are the words which thou shalt speak unto the children of Israel. — Exodus 19:5, 6. And ye shall be holy unto me: for I the Lord am holy, and have severed you from other people, that ye should be mine.—Leviticus 20:26.

I will say to the north, Give up; and to the south, Keep not back: bring my sons from far, and my daughters from the ends of the earth: Even everyone that is called by my name.—Isaiah 43:6, 7.

> "He will gather, He will gather
> The gems for His kingdom;
> All the pure ones, all the bright ones,
> His loved and His own."

His Jewels

How does He keep His jewels? In the twenty-eighth chapter of Exodus, we read of twelve precious stones, representing all God's people, set in the breastplate of the High Priest, which he bore upon his breast continually. They were hidden there. "Your life is hid with Christ in God."—Colossians 3:3.

Borne on his heart they were represented at the mercy seat, and entered with him into the holiest place. Having therefore, brethren, boldness to enter into the holiest by the blood of Jesus, by a new and living way, which He hath consecrated for us, through the vail, that is to say, His flesh; and having an high priest over the house of God; let us draw near with a true heart in full assurance of faith, having our hearts sprinkled from an evil conscience, and our bodies washed with pure water. Let us hold fast the profession of our faith without wavering; for He is faithful that promised.—Hebrews 10: 19-23.

The high priest also had the names of the twelve tribes in jewels on his shoulder, which signifies the place of power. The Lord's own, His chosen ones, are carried on His heart of love, and on His shoulder of strength. I love to repeat the true story of poor Jack, who, without ordinary earthly wisdom, had learned much of the wisdom of heaven. He was dying, and one who had always been a good friend to him asked him if he was afraid. "Oh, no, not the least afraid," he said.—"Why, have you never done anything bad, Jack?" "Oh, yes, much bads," he said. "God had a whole page against him. But when he first prayed to Jesus, He took the book out of God's hands and drew His own pierced hand over the page so that every sin was blotted out, and God could see nothing but Jesus' blood. And when he came to stand before Him, while He held the book up to the sun, God would say, ' No, nothing there against

Jack.' Then God would shut the book and the Lord Jesus Christ would come and put His arm around him and say, ' My Jack,' and bid him stand with the angels till the rest were judged."

Verily, verily, I say unto you, He that heareth my word, and believeth on Him that sent me, hath everlasting life, and shall not come into condemnation; but is passed from death unto life.—John 5 : 24. In whom ye also trusted, after that ye heard the word of truth, the gospel of your salvation: in whom also, after that ye believed, ye were sealed with that Holy Spirit of promise, which is the earnest of our inheritance until the redemption of the purchased possession, unto the praise of His glory.—Ephesians 1 : 13.

It is, then, a matter of great moment to be sure that we are among the sealed ones; genuine jewels that will stand any test.

Then shall ye return, and discern between the righteous and the wicked, between him that serveth God and him that serveth Him not.—Malachi 3:18.

There is a difference, eternal, unchangeable, between those who are only God's professed children and God's own. Jesus answered, Verily, verily, I say unto thee, Except a man be born of water and of the Spirit, he cannot enter the kingdom of God. That which is born of the flesh is flesh; and that which is born of the Spirit is spirit. Marvel not that I said unto thee, Ye must be born again. The wind bloweth where it listeth, and thou hearest the sound thereof, but canst not tell whence it cometh, and whither it goeth: so is everyone that is born of the Spirit. —John 3:5-7.

Every kind of gem has been imitated to such a degree of similarity that even the most experienced eye can only detect the difference by the closest scrutiny. But

His Jewels

there is a lack of hardness and permanency in the artificial gems which, after a time, shows their true character. And there are tests known to the dealers which readily distinguish gem from gem, the true from the false—the God-made jewel from the man-made imitation. *Every man's work shall be made manifest: for the day shall declare it, because it shall be revealed by fire; and the fire shall try every man's work of what sort it is.*—1 Corinthians 3: 13.

A lady dropped a ring with a valuable jewel in the open fire. The next day from the dead ashes the gem was raked out, unharmed. The setting had melted in the heat, the gem was unhurt. When thou, if a true jewel, passest through the fire, thou shalt not be burned, neither shall the flames kindle upon thee. But how much more blessed is it to have not only the gem itself spared, but the setting also; to have gold, silver, and precious stones in the work we do for Him whose we are and whom we serve!

Thou canst not tell the mystery of the new birth which marks the true jewels of the Lord.

Men have sought to discover Nature's secret in transforming so homely and dark a substance as charcoal into a beautiful and brilliant diamond, but they cannot even learn from what department of Nature's laboratory it comes, or what the chemical conditions that secure it. So is it with the Lord's jewels. Even the mystery which hath been hid from ages and from generations, but now is made manifest to His saints: to whom God would make known what is the riches of the glory of this mystery among the Gentiles; which is Christ in you, the hope of glory.—Colossians 1:26, 27.

It is His own blessed secret which He tells only to those who believe, in simple faith and love.

His Jewels

Much research has been given not only to find out the mystery of how the diamond is made, but also to imitate it. But in the nearest approach to it, there is yet lacking that indiscoverable something which gives it its unrivaled preciousness.

The finest gems are often found looking like rough pebbles, and it requires the lapidary's art to bring out their beauty, and to fit them to their proper setting.

The process is something like this. The rough stone is embedded in cement, and a dull-edged diamond is rubbed across the surface, so as to leave an indentation that determines the line of cleavage. The operation is then repeated with a diamond having a slightly sharper edge, and finally with one as keen as a razor. A marked depression is thus made, into which a sharp steel knife is inserted. A quick and light blow divides the stone into two parts. The next process is known as that of cutting, an operation during which the stone is given its general form. A factory in St. Louis possesses a machine never before used in America, and only recently adopted by a few of the largest establishments in Europe. Instead of following the old method of rubbing two stones together by hand, the stone undergoing treatment is inserted in the chuck of a lathe revolving at a high rate of speed, and is placed in contact with another diamond that is likewise fastened in an adjustable chuck held in the hand of the operator. In the course of this operation the stone receives its form and outline. This process secures a much better result than could be obtained by the old method. The powder which results from the stones rubbing against each other is used later in polishing.

The stone is then ready for the polisher. He must first determine the character he will give the diamond, and select the

His Jewels

method of working it. He inserts the stone in a conical mass of molten lead, allowing a particular section to remain exposed. As soon as the lead has hardened, the polisher places the stone upon his wheel, which rotates at the rate of twenty-three hundred revolutions per minute. As the position of each diamond is changed in the setting from twenty-five to thirty times, an idea of the number of operations required before the stone is properly faceted may be had. Having arrived at a certain stage, the stone is sent back to the cutter that he may remove any sharp edges or irregularities produced during the process of polishing. At his hands, also, the stone receives its perfectly rounded form, after which it is returned to the polisher, who gives it its finishing touches. It is interesting to note that a given parcel of rough goods is kept intact throughout the entire process, the product being retained as one parcel. It may start at one thousand carats of rough goods, and go through all the operations until it appears as a parcel of gems weighing perhaps no more than three hundred and fifty carats, varying in size and quality, but all derived from the original parcel.

The analogy is suggestive.

Behold, I have refined thee, but not with silver; I have chosen thee in the furnace of affliction.—Isaiah 48:10. I will be glad and rejoice in Thy mercy: for Thou hast considered my trouble; Thou hast known my soul in adversities. —Psalm 31:7. For Thou, O God, hast proved us: Thou hast tried us, as silver is tried. Thou broughtest us into the net; Thou laidst affliction upon our loins. Thou hast caused men to ride over our heads; we went through fire and through water: but Thou broughtest us out into a wealthy place.—Psalm 66:10-12.

In preparing the gem, it is said the

His Jewels

plan must be perfectly understood by the artist at the commencement of his work. No careless, haphazard cutting here and there will do. So it is with His jewels.

For I know the thoughts that I think toward you, saith the Lord, thoughts of peace, and not of evil, to give you an expected end.—Jeremiah 29:11. And I will bring the third part through the fire, and will refine them as silver is refined, and will try them as gold is tried: they shall call on my name, and I will hear them: I will say, It is my people: and they shall say, The Lord is my God.—Zech. 13:9.

Here we are, rough diamonds, embedded in this commonplace life for a purpose. To find the cleavage plane where, with infinite skill, the divine fashioner of our character will begin His work, He uses some dull-edged diamond, a fellow diamond, some inefficient person who seems to prevent our getting on in life, some circumstance, disappointment, commonplace test, the thousand and one things which try every life, and which we refer to second causes, forgetting the "dull diamond" is in the hand of a skillful designer. But the cleavage plane is discovered, and a keener trial comes to mark it still more plainly. Then the sharp knife of an experience keener still, then the quick, decisive blow—a change in all the relations of life, a dividing asunder of every plan and purpose; a cruel blow, we say, but it is the only way to put the diamond where it can be shaped and polished for its final glorious setting. It is said the workman must know perfectly the position of what is called the cleavage planes, as it is only upon them the pieces can be removed with the chisel without injury to the jewel; that is, he must know where to strike. The lapidary takes up the rough stone, knowing he has a treasure if it can be properly developed. To let it remain in its rough condition would be to cut off its possibilities; it must be brought out, cut, polished, set, in order to find its highest value.

O Lord, Thou hast searched me, and known me. Thou knowest my downsitting and mine uprising, Thou understandest my thought afar off. Thou compassest my path and my lying down, and art acquainted with all my ways. For there is not a word in my tongue, but, lo, O Lord, Thou knowest it altogether. Thou hast beset me behind and before, and laid Thine hand upon me. Thine eyes did see my substance, yet being unperfect; and in Thy book all my members were written, which in continuance were fashioned, when as yet there was none of them. How precious also are Thy thoughts unto me, O God! how great is the sum of them! If I should count them, they are more in number than the sand: when I awake, I am still with Thee. Search me, O God, and know my heart: try me, and know my thoughts: and see if there be any wicked way in me, and lead me in the way everlasting.—Psalm 139: 1-5; 16-18; 23, 24.   But Thou, O Lord, knowest me: Thou hast tried my heart toward Thee.—Jer. 12: 3.

Oh, those cleavage planes in us! How well the Lord knows where to cut His loved and His own, though the cleavage plane may be where we least think it is!

Right where natural affection bleeds the most; where pride, not necessarily sinful pride either, cries out most sorely, where the joints and marrow of this soul redeemed by Him will part—there His strong, steady, unflinching hand cuts and forms the jewel for the setting designed by Him for it, where the designer's skill and its own beauty will be best set forth.

The lapidary's apparatus for cutting, grinding, and polishing is made of the most common materials, lead, pewter, brass, iron, and soft alloys. So some of the Lord's most precious jewels are being fitted for their final setting by the commonest and most prosaic circumstances of daily life and toil. There comes to be a heroism in great suffering that relieves it of part of its sting. But there is no heroism about the sting of a nettle bush, nor is there any, to our eyes, in the petty annoyances of our daily life. Yet it is here the greater part of His jewels are cut and shaped and polished.

Having found the lines on which to work out the best results for the gem, the next process is that of cutting. They used to rub two stones together to give each jewel its form; but methods change in cutting both the material and the spiritual diamond. Still, it is the other diamond which is the instrument, and the hand of the designer directs the process just the same. The new process has a diamond inserted in a lathe going by machinery at a high rate of speed; another diamond is fastened in an adjustable chuck, or grip, held in the hand of the operator. We live in the whirr and whizz of busy years. We are cut and ground by contact with men and women in the rush of life, but the hand of the operator guides, and the plan for each diamond is clear in His mind.

> " And so I whisper, 'As God will,'
> And in His mighty hand hold still."

The lapidary's table has a groove around it to preserve the pieces of the jewel, its very dust, to use in polishing other gems. As the pieces fly off, well might the jewel exclaim, could it speak, " To what purpose is this waste ? " But the cutter understands, and no part is wasted. So with His jewels. As the self-will, the ambitions, the sharp edges of our character, are cut and shaped by the circumstances of our life, circumstances which we misunderstand so completely that we say, "There must be some mistake," the careful cutter of His jewel is ever using the seeming waste to polish others of His gems.

How little we know our influence over others! The self-restraint in the home, under provocation; the patient forbearance, the denial of self, the little acts of love, and the little words—all the process of our fitting for His final setting—we know not how much it is doing for other gems that will shine beside us in His crown forever. Have you not watched some patient sufferer and felt your own impatience rebuked and your faith strengthened? Be encouraged; your own cutting is going to polish and beautify somebody else as well as yourself.

While the lapidary cuts, he examines with a magnifying glass, and occasionally takes a proof of his work in wax. That the trial [or proof] of your faith, being much more precious than of gold that perisheth, though it be tried with fire, might be found unto praise and honor and glory at the appearing of Jesus Christ. —1 Peter 1 : 7.

We often mistake or overestimate our faith, or we may underestimate it. God sends a fiery trial to prove it. Let us be patient; He tests, because He will have us perfect.

Some gems cut very slowly, and the process is a delicate one. The sapphire is one of the most precious jewels, and it cuts perhaps most slowly of all, but presents beautifully smooth surfaces when done. Precious jewel of the Saviour's treasure, be not disheartened if it seems the process is slow, and the jewel unyielding. Hold still in the lapidary's hand. Perhaps you will be among His brightest by and by.

It is the custom in Brazil to liberate the slave who finds a diamond of a certain weight when gathering them from

His Jewels

the river beds. Think of his joy when he receives this reward for his search. And they that be wise shall shine as the brightness of the firmament; and they that turn many to righteousness, as the stars for ever and ever.—Daniel 12:3. So let him know, that he which converteth the sinner from the error of his way shall save a soul from death, and shall hide a multitude of sins.—James 5:20. For what is our hope, or joy, or crown of rejoicing? Are not even ye in the presence of our Lord Jesus Christ at His coming? For ye are our glory and joy.—1 Thessalonians 2:19.

There is no joy on earth equal to the joy of gathering gems for the Saviour's crown. The Princess Eugenie of Sweden, a woman noted for her benevolence, found it necessary to add a ward to a hospital in which she was interested. Not having the money at command, she sold her jewels for this purpose.

One day, in passing through this ward, a pale sufferer lying upon one of the neat little beds stretched out her hand to the Princess as she passed, and with tears shining in her eyes she said: " Oh, Princess, had it not been for you, I would never have had this comfort and care." And the Princess said: " I have found my diamonds in the tears of this grateful woman." Diamonds are lovely, especially so because they are the work of God; but if my possessing even one would rob His treasury of that which I ought to give in order that His immortal jewels may be won, far rather let me choose to find my jewels as the Princess found hers.

Precious stones possess a hardness which renders them susceptible to the highest polish, and capable of retaining the forms into which they are cut, and the figures that may be engraved on them. The ancient artists had each his peculiar

His Jewels

cipher which he put upon the gem. Connoisseurs can refer each gem to its period, country, and artist. Him that overcometh will I make a pillar in the temple of my God, and he shall go no more out: and I will write upon him the name of my God, and the name of the city of my God, which is new Jerusalem, which cometh down out of heaven from my God: and I will write upon him my new name.—Revelation 3:12. To him that overcometh will I give a white stone, and in the stone a new name written, which no man knoweth saving he that receiveth it.—Revelation 2:17. And the Gentiles shall see thy righteousness, and all kings thy glory: and thou shalt be called by a new name, which the mouth of the Lord shall name. Thou shalt also be a crown of beauty in the hand of the Lord, and a royal diadem in the hand of thy God.—Isaiah 62:2, 3.

And the Lord their God shall save

them in that day as the flock of His people; for they shall be as the stones of a crown, lifted up as an ensign upon His land.—Zechariah 9:16. On His head were many crowns.—Revelation 19:12. Then shall the righteous shine forth as the sun in the kingdom of their Father. —Matthew 13:43.

His jewels are upon His heart now, they will be in His crown then.

> " When the Lord makes up His jewels,
>   Choosing gems of every hue ;
> Pearls and diamonds, rubies, sapphires,
>   Showing flawless through and through,
> Could I be the least among them,
>   Smallest gem that love could see,
> And His eye detect the brightness,
>   That would be enough for me.
>
> Precious stones are cut and polished
>   By the lapidary's skill ;
> Cruel knife and rasping friction
>   Work on each the Master's will.
> Not until the sparkling facets
>   With an equal luster glow,
> Does the artist choose a setting
>   For the gem perfected so.

His Jewels

"Thus I wait the royal pleasure,
    And, when trouble comes to me,
Smile, to think He may be working
    On the gem, though small it be.
All I ask is strength to bear it,
    Faith and patience to be still :
Held by Him, no knife can slay me ;
    Loving Him, no anguish kill."

THE HEART'S STORY.

I will not doubt, though all my ships at sea
    Come drifting home, with broken masts and sails;
    I will believe the Hand that never fails,
From seeming evil, worketh good for me;
And, though I weep because those sails are tattered,
Still will I cry, while my best hopes lie shattered,
        "I trust in Thee."

I will not doubt, though all my prayers return
    Unanswered from the still, white realm above;
    I will believe it is an all-wise love
Which has refused these things for which I yearn;
And, though at times I cannot keep from grieving,
Yet the pure ardor of my fixed believing
        Undimmed shall burn.

I will not doubt, though sorrows fall like rain,
    And troubles swarm like bees about to hive;
    I will believe the heights for which I strive
Are only reached by anguish and by pain;
And, though I groan and writhe beneath my crosses,
I yet shall see through my severest losses
        The greater gain.

I will not doubt. Well anchored in this faith,
    Like some stanch ship, my soul braves every gale,
    So strong its courage will not quail
To breast the mighty unknown sea of death.
Oh, may I cry, though body parts with spirit,
"I do not doubt," so listening worlds may hear it,—
        With my last breath!

Selected.

October

Things Working for Good

And we know that all things work together for good to them that love God, to them who are the called according to His purpose.—Romans 8 : 28.

"AND we know." Oh, what a comfort to be *sure!* In the midst of so much that is dark and doubtful, how like a bright clear patch of blue in the troubled sky is St. Paul's cheerful " we know "! It will clear off sometime. Weeping may endure for the night, but joy cometh in the morning. It is always morning somewhere, even on this earth; it is always morning everywhere with God. God is light, and in Him is no darkness at all (1 John 1 : 5); and the way out of our darkness is to find God. " And there shall be no night" when fully He the work hath wrought that caused our needless fear.

How does St. Paul know that all things work together for good to them that love God? Does it look so? Did it look as if things were prosperous and hopeful for him when he wrote:

We are troubled on every side, yet not distressed; we are perplexed, but not in despair.—2 Corinthians 4:8. Of the Jews five times received I forty stripes save one. Thrice was I beaten with rods, once was I stoned, thrice I suffered shipwreck, a night and a day I have been in the deep; in journeyings often, in perils of waters, in perils of robbers, in perils by my own countrymen, in perils by the heathen, in perils in the city, in perils in the wilderness, in perils in the sea, in perils among false brethren; in weariness and painfulness, in watchings often, in hunger and thirst, in fastings

Things Working for Good

often, in cold and nakedness. Beside those things that are without, that which cometh upon me daily, the care of all the churches.—2 Cor. 11 : 24–28.

The very same sorrows, perplexities, disappointments, were in his own life and in the lives of his friends as we experience now. And yet he said without hesitation or qualification : " We know that all things work together for good to them that love God." I am sure we very much need the comfort and strength of such a settled belief as this. Nothing helps so much in the battle of life as a cheerful courage; discouragement takes the nerve out of us, and hinders success. A buoyant spirit tones the whole being and makes us press on to victory. And what a solid basis for courage in the midst of difficulties is the assurance that things are surely coming out right at last! You could hopefully and cheerfully watch for weeks beside one suffering with illness if you were sure that the fever, the pain, the uncomfortable remedies, were working together toward an outcome of stronger health and vigor than the sufferer had ever known before.

I think there were three ways by which St. Paul, under the guidance of the Holy Spirit, arrived at this satisfactory and inspiring conclusion. First, I think he came to it logically by his process of reasoning, which makes this book of Romans, especially this eighth chapter, so rich and full of meat. Second, he came to it through the emphatic declarations of this blessed Word, all of which he believed had been given by inspiration of God; and third, he came to it through his own experience. Now, if you and I can come for ourselves to the same satisfactory conclusion—not to a theory, not a hearsay, but to our own calm, settled, happy assurance that, no matter how things look, they truly are working to-

Things Working for Good

gether for our good, then we will be ready to join in the pæan of rejoicing which bursts from the soul of the apostle when he cries out in verses 31–39:

What shall we then say to these things? If God be for us, who can be against us? He that spared not His own Son, but delivered Him up for us all, how shall He not with Him also freely give us all things? Who shall lay anything to the charge of God's elect? It is God that justifieth. Who is he that condemneth? It is Christ that died, yea rather, that is risen again, who is even at the right hand of God, who also maketh intercession for us. Who shall separate us from the love of Christ? shall tribulation, or distress, or persecution, or famine, or nakedness, or peril, or sword? As it is written, For Thy sake we are killed all the day long; we are accounted as sheep for the slaughter. Nay, in all these things we are more than conquerors through Him that loved us. For

I am persuaded, that neither death, nor life, nor angels, nor principalities, nor powers, nor things present, nor things to come, nor height, nor depth, nor any other creature, shall be able to separate us from the love of God, which is in Christ Jesus our Lord.

I saw a little child on the train just before we entered the tunnel. Her father knew she would be afraid in the dark, and he lifted her out of her seat into his arms. When we came out into the sunlight, she was gazing in his face with an intense look of inquiry—a mingling of fear and trust; then she broke out in a smile that said so much! The tunnel had been dark, she did not enjoy it, but she was quiet through it because her father held her. When she came again into the sunlight, she saw his face; she knew he had kept her safe, she answered his smile with a glad acknowledgment, and all the while the passage through the tunnel brought

Things Working for Good

her nearer the place where she wanted to go. Her father knew this while they were in the darkness; baby did not know it then, but she was quiet in his arms. Let us enter the kingdom of God " as a little child."

We often hear this passage quoted in a way foreign to its meaning. People say: " Oh! I hope all things will work for good. I am sure they ought to for so-and-so, for she surely loves God;" or, " I think all things are working for good," meaning they hope or believe that things will come out as they want them. But it is not said we know that. In fact, we know just the opposite. We know that some of God's dear children meet with great disappointments. They lose their money, they suffer pain, they have sorrows that cut to their very heart's core. Things do not come out as they would choose at all.

Consequently in that way of looking

they do not work for good, but just the reverse.

Nor does the text say, We know all things work for good to everybody. They would, if God could have His way with everybody. He is not willing that any should perish, but rather that all should turn unto Him and live. Oh! the meaning of that word perish, the fullness of that word live! But if we will not fall in with His plan for us, how can He do us the good He would?

Thus, you have a child who is very dear to you. You have great plans for his future, and you are ready to put everything you have at his disposal for his advantage. But he will not be in sympathy with your purpose; he has plans of his own which he is determined to carry out. You know they will result in disaster, but you cannot persuade him to your way of thinking. Things do not work for his good as you had intended

Things Working for Good

they should. But it is his fault, not yours. So it is with ourselves and God. If we love God, we are in sympathy with His thought for us, so that all His resources are at our disposal; He can make everything turn to our advantage because we fall in with His way, which is the way of wisdom and of love.

But, on the other hand, do you say sadly: "I am afraid I do not love Him as I ought, and the assurance is not for me?" Hear Him saying: He that is not against me is for me. The bruised reed He will not break. The willing and obedient shall eat the good of the land.

St. Paul says very decidedly, all things work for good. You cannot get outside of God's all, so let us go the way he went, and see if we can come out at the same delightful resting-place. When we look into the Word to see what Christ does for us, and in us, what treasures of infinite love are unfolded to us! How plainly we see that from pure love for us He gave Himself to redeem us from the curse of sin, and settled forever the question of our complete rescue from the power and dominion of evil.

Who hath delivered us from the power of darkness, and hath translated us into the kingdom of His dear Son: in whom we have redemption through His blood, even the forgiveness of sins. And you, that were sometime alienated and enemies in your mind by wicked works, yet now hath He reconciled in the body of His flesh through death, to present you holy and unblamable and unreprovable in His sight: if ye continue in the faith grounded and settled, and be not moved away from the hope of the gospel, which ye have heard, and which was preached to every creature which is under heaven; whereof I Paul am made a minister.—Colossians 1: 13, 14, 21–23.

Herein is love, not that we loved God,

Things Working for Good

but that He loved us, and sent His Son to be the propitiation for our sins.—1 John 4: 10.

Behold, what manner of love the Father hath bestowed upon us, that we should be called the sons of God: therefore, the world knoweth us not, because it knew Him not. Beloved, now are we the sons of God, and it doth not yet appear what we shall be: but we know that, when He shall appear, we shall be like Him; for we shall see Him as He is.—1 John 3: 1, 2.

Being filled with the fruits of righteousness, which are by Jesus Christ, unto the glory and praise of God. — Philippians 1 : 11.

But we all, with open face beholding as in a glass the glory of the Lord, are changed into the same image from glory to glory, even as by the Spirit of the Lord. —2 Corinthians 3 : 18.

There is therefore now no condemnation to them which are in Christ Jesus, who walk not after the flesh, but after the Spirit. For the law of the Spirit of life in Christ Jesus hath made me free from the law of sin and death.—Romans 8: 1, 2.

He has changed us into His own image, filled us with the fruits of righteousness by His Spirit, made us partakers of the divine nature, given us the spirit of adoption, put us where there is no condemnation against us, included even our bodies in His redemption, and given the Holy Spirit to help us in prayer.

Likewise the Spirit also helpeth our infirmities: for we know not what we should pray for as we ought: but the Spirit itself maketh intercession for us with groanings which cannot be uttered. And He that searcheth the hearts knoweth what is the mind of the Spirit, because He maketh intercession for the saints according to the will of God.—Romans 8: 26, 27.

So that even here in the flesh we can talk with God in a way pleasing to God.

Things Working for Good

No wonder St. Paul asks, What shall we say to these things ? Logically, there can be but one thing to say: He that spared not His own Son, but delivered Him up for us all, how shall He not with Him also freely give us all things ?—Romans 8 : 32.

If our Father has a purpose to conform us to the image of His Son, so that we may bear the family likeness and be in full accord with all the interests, pursuits, enjoyments, comforts, and share in all the possessions of the family ("of whom the whole family in heaven and earth is named"), there is but one conclusion to reach: everything in His providence must work into this plan. No matter how adverse it seems, it must contribute to the final outcome of His purpose for good. Added to this logical conclusion is the testimony of God's Word, in illustration and promise.

The steps of a good man are ordered by

the Lord: and he delighteth in His way. Though he fall, he shall not be utterly cast down: for the Lord upholdeth him with His hand.—Psalm 37: 23, 24.

For the Lord God is a sun and shield: the Lord will give grace and glory: no good thing will He withhold from them that walk uprightly.—Psalm 84: 11.

Although the fig tree shall not blossom, neither shall fruit be in the vines; the labor of the olive shall fail, and the fields shall yield no meat; the flocks shall be cut off from the fold, and there shall be no herd in the stalls: yet will I rejoice in the Lord, I will joy in the God of my salvation. Jehovah, the Lord, is my strength, and He maketh my feet like hinds' feet, and will make me to walk upon mine high places.—Habakkuk 3: 17–19.

For the Lamb which is in the midst of the throne shall feed them, and shall lead them unto living fountains of waters: and God shall wipe away all tears from their eyes.—Revelation 7: 17. This is simply because there never will be anything any more to make us weep. All things in life—this life redeemed by the precious blood of Jesus, and transformed by the Holy Spirit—shall be for His praise and glory, and for our good for ever and ever.

Jacob was far from perfect, but he was God's child, and God made the very worst things in his life turn to his advantage. Do you say, then, that sin can ever be a force working for good ? Not sin persisted in, but sin repented of and forsaken, can. St. Paul was the more humble and loving because he remembered how he had persecuted the Lord Jesus. " I am not worthy to be called an apostle. I am less than the least of all saints because I persecuted the church of God." Peter wrote, with a power that goes to the heart, of the glory of being a partaker with Christ's sufferings, and bearing reproach for His name, because he had once known the shame of denying Him. Mary loved much, because she had much forgiven. A wonderful Saviour is ours! We are more than conquerors through Him that loved us. My sins, my follies, my mistakes, I will put entirely into His hands. I do not see how it can be done, but Love has wondrous power. He will transmute and transform all, so that even these dark threads shall become golden in the fabric of my character.

It is said in Psalm 105:19, that God's Word tried Joseph. So it tries us. Has God forgotten? Is He slack concerning His promise? The circumstances of Joseph's life seemed to contradict God's Word, and to render its fulfillment impossible. Cast into a pit, sold into slavery, thrown into prison, yet these very circumstances were working together to fulfill God's plan for him. The story was written that we, through comfort of the Scriptures, might have hope. Jacob said:

Things Working for Good

"All these things are against me," when his sons went to Egypt with Benjamin; but when they returned with such wonderful tidings he exclaimed: "It is enough, it is enough!"

> "To have each day the things I wish,
>   Lord, seemeth best to me;
> But not to have some things I wish,
>   Lord, seemeth best to Thee.
>
> "Henceforth then let Thy will be done!
>   Though mine, O God, be crossed;
> 'T is good to see my plans o'erthrown,
>   Myself in Thee all lost."

"Really no one understands about it, and I have no one to talk with but just God Himself." For the moment it seemed to us a hard experience for the earnest woman who uttered these words with tears in her eyes; but upon second thought we knew that it was one of the blessed "all things" working "for good." We knew it not as a matter of theory, nor even of faith, for it impressed itself in the face and tone, and in the evidently maturing character of the speaker.

We get our best things directly from God. Human friendships, the communion of saints, and the stimulus to spiritual life which comes from association are greatly to be valued; but we learn best as private pupils in personal intercourse with the divine teacher. It is said of Mary that she " sat at Jesus' feet, and kept listening to His word." Doubtless she often repeated to her sister Martha the things she heard, but they could never have come to her with the force and stimulus with which they fell upon Mary's ear directly from the lips of Jesus.

It is not so much in the great events of life that we learn this precious lesson of companionship with God. There are sorrows in some lives which are like lonely mountain fastnesses, where, in hours apart with Him, the soul has had unutterable revelations. But the daily routine, " the common round," has its lonely places, too, where only God understands. If we should speak of the trial to another, the reply might come: " Why do you care ? such things do not trouble me."—" True, but you are different. I see you cannot understand "; and we turn away disappointed. But if to the Friend unfailing we have learned to go, and

> " Tell Him everything
> As it rises,
> And at once to Him to bring
> All surprises,"

how soon we find He does understand, and His peace keeps heart and mind as in a strong fortress.

Nor, to go a step further, does this feeling of being understood by God only, lead to a misanthropic spirit. It does not recoil like the sensitive plant from all human touch, but rather, from the divine companionship it learns the charity which "never faileth, hopeth all things, believeth all things, suffers long, and is kind." Taking daily experiences in this way, we may truly "in everything give thanks."

Some of the hills of life are very steep and rugged. We can only mount them as we hold fast to our Guide. We shall slip, slip down into hopelessness and despair unless we hold fast to the strong assurance of Him whose word faileth never. "All things work together for good to them that love God."

This delightful assurance of St. Paul grew also out of his own experience.

And lest I should be exalted above measure through the abundance of the revelations, there was given to me a thorn in the flesh, the messenger of Satan to buffet me, lest I should be exalted above measure. For this thing I besought the Lord thrice, that it might depart from

Things Working for Good

me. And He said unto me, My grace is sufficient for thee: for my strength is made perfect in weakness. Most gladly therefore will I rather glory in my infirmities, that the power of Christ may rest upon me. Therefore I take pleasure in infirmities, in reproaches, in necessities, in persecutions, in distresses for Christ's sake: for when I am weak, then am I strong.—2 Corinthians 12 : 7–10.

Never shall I forget a day when in sorrow because a dear little child had been taken from our household, and in great physical pain, I sat alone in a darkened room. My hands were so disabled that I could scarcely turn the leaves of my Bible, but it opened to these verses. With a sudden flash-light the Holy Spirit poured them upon my soul's vision. The loss, the pain, the loneliness, were heavy, but the strength made perfect in weakness, the power of Christ resting upon me, more than made up for all. I understood then, in a little measure, Paul's testimony to the sweetness of most bitter things.

And, as if imprisonment, persecution, and all the rest which had befallen this brave, true servant of God were not enough, shipwreck must follow! Really it looked as if God did not take care of him at all. But Paul knew better. He had learned the best lesson one can learn —to trust God perfectly, no matter how things look. So when there was great confusion on the ship, some advised one thing and some another, and all were so frightened they could not eat, Paul was perfectly quiet and begged them to take food. "Do not throw yourselves into the sea," he said; "stay in the ship and you will all be safe, for He whose I am and whom I serve has told me I must go to Rome, and that all in the ship with me shall be saved. And I believe God that it shall be even as it was told me. 'Thou wilt keep him in perfect peace whose mind is stayed on Thee, because he trusteth in Thee.'"—Isaiah 26: 3.

Moon and stars did not appear; the sea was high; the ship finally went to pieces. But Paul paid no attention to appearances, and went on believing God. So he was not only quiet himself, but he could cheer up others. It is blessed to believe God. It is the only way to keep a cheerful, courageous heart when things seem to be going to pieces as they often do, like a tempest-driven vessel.

One day Mr. Spurgeon came in, saying to his deacons, "Brethren, I am fresh from a struggle with doubts." "And why," said one of the deacons, "did you not tell us you were fresh from a struggle to keep from horse-stealing?" "What do you mean?" asked Mr. Spurgeon. "Well, the same God that forbids your stealing a horse, also forbids your doubting. How dare you do the one more than the other?" "You are right,"

Mr. Spurgeon said, "I have no more right to doubt God than I have to steal a horse."

How should you feel if one should question any promise you should make? Why, then, should you question anything which God has told you? Paul believed "even as it was told him," not as he thought it ought to be, or as it looked as if it might be, but as God said it should be. So we must believe His Word. He tells me He loves me. I must believe the love, and trust Him as my Father. Like myriads of stars in the sky, the promises of God shine in His Word. Let us believe even as it is told us, then we shall be happy, calm, and full of courage, and can say to the troubled, fearful ones around us, "Be of good cheer." What a comfort to have a man like St. Paul on board ship in a storm! How glad we are to meet men and women of faith when we are in trouble, doubt, or distress! If you would be helpful to others you must yourself believe God even as it is told you.

Sir George Matheson of Scotland is totally blind, yet one of the most learned and gifted men in all Britain, and a magnetic orator. Though always in total darkness, he is a cheerful, happy-hearted Christian. He has written this: " My God, I have never thanked Thee for my thorn. I have thanked Thee a thousand times for my roses, but not once for my thorn. I have been looking forward to a world where I shall get compensation for my cross, but I have never thought of my cross as itself a present glory. Thou Divine Love, whose human path has been perfected through sufferings, teach me the glory of my cross; teach me the value of my thorn. Show me that I have climbed to Thee by the path of pain. Show me that my tears have made my rainbow. Reveal to me that my strength was the product of the thorn when I wrestled until the break of day. Then shall I know that my thorn was sent by Thee."

"How shall I quiet my heart? how shall I keep it still?
   How shall I hush its tremulous start at tidings of
      good or ill?

"How shall I gather and hold contentment and peace
      and rest,
   Wrapping their sweetness fold on fold over my
      troubled breast?

"The Spirit of God is still and gentle and mild and
      sweet,
   What time His omnipotent glorious will guideth the
      worlds at His feet.

"Controlling all lesser things, this turbulent heart of
      mine
   He keepeth as under His folded wings, in a peace
      serene, divine.

"So shall I quiet my heart, so shall I keep it still,
   So shall I hush its tremulous start at tidings of good
      or ill;

"So shall I silence my soul with a peacefulness deep
      and broad;
   So shall I gather divine control in the infinite quiet
      of God."

A DAY OF GOLD.

Quiet and peace, heart's-ease and delight,
Autumnal sky, hill, valley,—and night !

Heaven bends tenderly near to bless
The earth, with kisses of chaste caress,

Soothing her into satisfied rest,
A trustful heart on a lover's breast.

In tinted foliage night winds sigh
Answers of love to the bending sky ;

Earth has forgotten—a little while—
To-morrow's summons to grief and toil.

She rests, and has all her heart can take
Of heaven, lavished for love's sweet sake.

Till the voice of morning, low and clear—
Voice that is silence to human ear—

Gives speech ; and then earth expectant waits
The sun to ride through his royal gates,

And the story of her hope is told
As he covers her with flaming gold !

Truth revealed in autumn's day of gold
Is new-born—as eternity old.

Rest, then, and have all the heart can take
Of heaven, lavished for Christ's dear sake,

To keep content through expectant night
Lives that shall wake to immortal light.

E. J. K.

November

Upon My Watch-Tower

I will stand upon my watch, and set me upon the tower, and will watch to see what He will say unto me, and what I shall answer when I am reproved.—Hab. 2 : 1.

IN the days of the prophet, the long-ago years of the world, nations and tribes and men were on the defensive against each other constantly. They expected to be beset by enemies, and all their cities and villages were built with a view to protection. High walls surrounded most of them, and here and there upon the walls or on some near outpost were built watch-towers, where the watchman kept guard, and was ready to sound the alarm at the first approach of a foe. In those far-away days, there were no methods of communication except the slow messenger upon horse or foot, and the business of the watchman upon the tower was to catch the first signal of communication and pass it on to those who waited for it.

We do not live in fear of outward foes. For we wrestle not against flesh and blood, but against principalities, against powers, against the rulers of the darkness of this world, against spiritual wickedness in high places.—Eph. 6: 12.

> " Ne'er think the victory won,
> Nor lay thine armor down ;
> The work of faith will not be done
> Till thou obtain the crown."

And far more need is there of watchtowers for knowledge of the foes of our spiritual life, for warning, for preparation against invasion, than there was need for them against the warriors of olden times.

The Bible is the book for all ages and all people. The prophet Habakkuk is filled with anxiety about the times in which he lives. He sees that violence, wrong, and injustice are everywhere, that men are selfish and care only for their own gains. And he foresees that a great enemy in the days to come will invade the land. He cries out in the most intense language to God: Lord, how long shall I cry, and Thou wilt not hear! even cry out unto Thee of violence, and Thou wilt not save!—Hab. 1:2.

The picture is very like what we see in these later days. Puzzling political and social questions; the distorted state of our own hearts; the mysterious ways of Providence; the questioning, How long? the pitiful or impatient Why? are agitating the world now as then. We say, one to another, I am your brother and companion in tribulation, and in the kingdom and patience of Jesus Christ. — Revelation 1:9. In his perplexity and inability to answer these questions, the prophet says he will do

Upon My Watch-Tower

just what we will have to do if we find rest for soul or wisdom for action. He will humbly wait upon God.

I will stand upon my watch, and set me upon the tower, and will watch to see what He will say unto me, and what I shall answer when I am reproved. And the Lord answered me, and said, Write the vision, and make it plain upon tables, that he may run that readeth it. For the vision is yet for an appointed time, but at the end it shall speak, and not lie; though it tarry, wait for it; because it will surely come, it will not tarry.—Hab. 2: 1-3.

I will stand upon my watch as a sentinel on the walls of a besieged city. As one anxious to gain intelligence I will look up, look out, look in. I will watch to see what He will say to, or in me, as the margin reads.

Take ye heed, watch and pray: for ye know not when the time is. For the Son of man is as a man taking a far journey, who left his house, and gave authority to his servants, and to every man his work, and commanded the porter to watch. Watch ye therefore: for ye know not when the master of the house cometh, at even, or at midnight, or at the cock-crowing, or in the morning: lest coming suddenly he find you sleeping. And what I say unto you I say unto all, Watch.—Mark 13: 33–37. Be sober, be vigilant; because your adversary the devil, as a roaring lion, walketh about, seeking whom he may devour: whom resist steadfast in the faith, knowing that the same afflictions are accomplished in your brethren that are in the world.—1 Peter 5: 8, 9.

It requires an ear intent to hear, a trained ear, else among the confusing voices we shall not recognize the One supreme voice, nor understand what is its word for us. Unto Thee lift I up mine eyes, O Thou that dwellest in the heavens.

Behold, as the eyes of servants look unto the hand of their masters, and as the eyes of a maiden unto the hand of her mistress; so our eyes wait upon the Lord our God, until that He have mercy upon us.—Psalm 123: 1, 2.

At the siege of Lucknow, when the English garrison was cut off from supplies, and in danger of massacre at the hands of the Sepoys, every eye and ear were strained to catch the first sign of Havelock's army coming to their relief. A Scotch girl, putting her ear close to the ground, caught the far-away strains of music, and springing up shouted, "Dinna ye hear the slogan?" sending a thrill of hope through every heart. So, with ear intent, the child of God may hear the Father's voice, for counsel and for comfort; and may hear, as others cannot hear, the tread of the coming Conqueror and Deliverer. I will stand upon my watch, and will watch to hear.

As in water face answereth to face, so the heart of man to man.—Proverbs 27:19. So by my own heart I know the need of yours. No need hath it so great as this—to hear and know and follow the voice of God. Does He really speak? Would He leave us in this wilderness alone? He will be very gracious unto thee at the voice of thy cry; when He shall hear it, He will answer thee. And though the Lord give you the bread of adversity, and the water of affliction, yet shall not thy teachers be removed into a corner any more, but thine eyes shall see thy teachers: and thine ears shall hear a word behind thee, saying, This is the way, walk ye in it, when ye turn to the right hand, and when ye turn to the left. —Isaiah 30:19-21.

To Him the porter openeth; and the sheep hear His voice: and He calleth His own sheep by name, and leadeth them out. And when He putteth forth His own sheep, He goeth before them, and the sheep follow Him: for they know His voice.—John 10: 3, 4.

We are in this world as one lost in a thicket. Those seeking us call and call again, but the rustle of our own footsteps prevents our hearing the voice of the rescuers. But we stop for a moment and stand silent; the distant voice reaches our ear; we listen; it comes again, nearer and nearer; we are sure now it is the voice of a friend. We answer; the quick response comes; we wait; they call; we answer; and soon the seeker and the sought come together in happy recognition.

So we wander, lost, bewildered, tired, hopeless. The sound of our own heartbeat, the clamor of the outside world, shut out the heavenly call, " Come unto me for rest." Sometimes the very importunity of our cry prevents our hearing the voice of the Lord. We must be silent to the Lord and wait patiently for Him.—Psalm 37: 7.

This word expresses an intent state of the soul. "I will set me upon my watch." I voluntarily place myself in a position to hear. I will stand with a fixed purpose, an alert attention, to wait for the message; not sitting listlessly, but looking out with eager expectation, and I must adjust my position so that obstructions will not hinder my hearing. What others say, my own ease, my own opinion, are very much in the way of my getting the exact meaning of what God would say to me. Rise up, ye women that are at ease; hear my voice, ye careless daughters. Give ear unto my speech. —Isaiah 32: 8, 9.

Who among you will give ear to this? Who will hearken and hear for the time to come?—Isaiah 42: 23. Hearken, O daughter, and consider, and incline thine ear.—Psalm 45: 10.

If thou forbear to deliver them that are drawn unto death, and those that are ready to be slain; if thou sayest, Behold, we knew it not; doth not He that pondereth the heart consider it? and He that keepeth thy soul, doth not He know it? and shall not He render to every man according to his works?—Proverbs 24: 11, 12.

I cannot excuse my indifference to the world's sin and sorrow by saying, "Behold, I knew it not." I must get upon my watch-tower by reading, hearing, and looking out for opportunities for service. The idea of a Christian not being intelligent upon the great questions of the day: the Sabbath; the legalizing of sin in any form; the crisis in missions; social reforms; and other things which make the world's heart beat fast these days!

Be thou instructed, O Jerusalem, lest my soul depart from thee; lest I make thee desolate, a land not inhabited. To whom shall I speak, and give warning, that they may hear? Behold, their ear is uncircumcised, and they cannot hearken: behold, the Word of the Lord is unto them a reproach: they have no delight in it. I have set thee for a tower and a fortress among my people, that thou mayest know and try their way.—Jeremiah 6: 8, 10, 27.

Especially should we, women, get upon our watch-tower, and listen very intently and reverently. "I have set thee for a tower and a fortress among my people." Never before did women hold such power and consequent responsibility for the world's moral and social condition; and the political which depends upon these. It is grand; but it is awfully solemn. There is a passage of the Word, lying far back among the shadows of Eden, which shows what is God's thought of woman as a coworker with Him in redemption. He said to the tempter, "I will put enmity between thee and the woman."

Satan's sharpest arrows have ever pierced her. God intends that she shall ever be preëminently his firm, determined, victorious enemy. This Scripture is fulfilled to-day in the organized efforts of women against vice of every kind; in her voice uplifted in all lands in behalf of the downtrodden and the sorrowful, and in favor of civil, social, and moral reform. "The conviction is growing, that it is high time for women who have been touched by the Spirit of Christ to awake to the perils and the possibilities of this magnificent age, and throw every energy of brain and heart into the business of filling the homes of this world with a new spirit and life." A man of wide observation has written these earnest words: "Would to God that some angel from His own right hand would reveal to woman the power she controls for the redemption of those horrible vices which defile and intoxicate the land! She should awe vice everywhere by the sternness of her disapproval. A divine trust is committed to her in her example and her very smiles, for which God will call her into judgment. I know that her sober rebuke may carry the power of many sermons to the heart and rescue a soul half lost, making her a minister of the cross."

We must get upon the watch-tower of the Word. We never can sufficiently emphasize the necessity of a simple-hearted study of the Bible in these perplexing days. When thou goest, it shall lead thee; when thou sleepest, it shall keep thee; and when thou wakest, it shall talk with thee. For the commandment is a lamp; and the law is light; and reproofs of instruction are the way of life. —Proverbs 6: 22, 23.

When thou awakest to thy duty, privilege, opportunity, it will talk with thee. Jesus said: " The words that I speak unto you, they are spirit, and they are life."

Bind them upon thy fingers, write them upon the tables of thine heart.—Proverbs 7 : 3.

No wonder we get mixed in our ideas of right and wrong, when we teach for doctrine the commandments of men.

What folly is it to allow the questioning spirit that is abroad to shake our faith in the living Word of God! Because the higher criticism demolishes some of the old human theories about this blessed book, shall that disturb our deep comfort in the spirit which giveth life ? The difficulty is, the masses of the people see only the troubled surface of those waters into whose depths devout thinkers are plunging. The little billows on the stream rock their lifeboats and they think a great wreck of everything is to follow. But the disturbance is only on the surface, and only for a time. The God of the Bible walks upon the waters, and He holds them in the hollow of His hand. No criticism yet has touched the living heart of this Word; not one principle, not one promise, not one law of conduct has ever changed in the least under the sharpest scrutiny of advanced scholarship. If the criticisms trouble us, it is probably because we cannot go into them deeply enough to understand them, and if we cannot, we had better turn away from them altogether, and hold fast the beginning of our confidence, steadfast unto the end. For if we let go of the old staff that has upheld us over many a rough way, in reaching after something we suppose will take its place, we will surely find that it is true of us as of God's people of old. "My people have committed two evils: they have forsaken me, the fountain of living waters; and they have hewed them out cisterns, broken cisterns that can hold no water." To whom shall we go? Thou hast the words of eternal life.

A traveler once, ascending a mountain,

said to his guide: "That point yonder looks like a glorious place for a broad outlook. Can I get up there?" The guide shook his head. "That, sir, is only for old travelers and steady nerves. If you were sure of holding tight to my stick, never letting go your grasp, and if you kept your head, it might pay you to go up there for what you might see. But if you should let go one instant, I should not like to answer for the consequences. I 've seen some sad results from making that attempt, sir." Let us hold fast to the dear old book, sure of seeing in it our Father's face and hearing His voice.

We must get upon our watch-tower of prayer.

Truly my soul waiteth upon God: from Him cometh my salvation. He only is my rock and my salvation; He is my defense; I shall not be greatly moved. My soul, wait thou only upon God, for all my expectation is from Him.—Psalm 62: 1-3.

They that wait, and expect from God, shall never be disappointed. The prayerful soul can say, " Mine ear hast Thou opened." Nothing is so sweet to hear as God's voice; to keep listening as did Mary, and not to be so cumbered with much serving that we cannot stop to listen. Sounds are confusing in this noisy, busy age. Let us watch to hear what God will say in us. We have no fear of the rushing billows when we hear Him saying, " It is I, be not afraid." We have courage to work when we hear Him saying, " Have not I sent thee ? I am with thee all the days." We can bear the trial when we hear Him saying that He will, with it, make a way of escape. The watch-tower of trial is one of the best of outlooks. " Couldst thou not watch with me one hour ? "

Write the vision, make it plain, that he may run that readeth it. Oh, how necessary for us, the children of our Father,

Upon My Watch-Tower

who have a sight of His face, to get us into our watch-tower and hear what He says, so that we may have something to tell plainly to others. Many are running to and fro; the rush of life is absorbing every energy; they do not take time to watch for themselves; we must hear for them. We must hear what He says about the clear and everlasting distinction between right and wrong, so that the force of our convictions may be strength for the indecision and weakness of those who are in danger of being swept down by the swift tide. Hear what He says about Christian work and giving, so that he who runs may read, in our example and our deep-settled purpose, the vision that we may not put into words. Hear what He says about being kept in perfect peace in Him. Not being careful and anxious, but trusting Him and believing all the unutterable assurances of His love and care, so that he who runs by us in the daily life may read it in the quiet brow, the calm and steady eyes, the spirit not of the world.

From questioning hearts everywhere comes to us the cry, Watchman, what of the night? O sad soul sitting in the shadow, the morning cometh, the calm, sweet dawn, the light of His face, the warmth, the growth, the promise of the day. Set thee upon thy tower, and hear His word of comfort, strength, and hope. What of the night? The night of the world's ignorance, sin, and unbelief? A dark night indeed, but the morning cometh. All the East is purple with the glory of the eternal Sun. Set thee upon thy watch-tower, O Christian. Observe the signs of the times—read, hear, and take thy place in the conquering ranks of the King. Let him that heareth run to tell, and though the vision tarry, wait, for it shall speak. "The just shall live by his faith."

There is a tower now in ruins in Pekin, called The Looking-toward-Home Tower. It was built nearly one hundred years ago by the Emperor for a favorite girl of his household. She pined for her home and her mother, and he had this tower built where she could look out toward her home, while from lower rooms there would ascend sounds of music that had been familiar to her there. Lonely, and sometimes homesick heart, set thee in thy watch-tower looking toward home. Read in the book, of the sinless, tearless, glorious city. Look until the vision is clear, the veil but dimly intervening. Listen until sweet home sounds rise above the discords of the near surroundings. Look, for the vision is yet for an appointed time, but at the end it shall speak, and not lie; though it tarry, wait for it; because it will surely come, it will not tarry. "I go to prepare a place for you, that where I am there you may be also."

THE VALLEY OF SILENCE.

I walk down the Valley of Silence,
   Down the dim, voiceless valley alone,
And I hear not the fall of a footstep
   Around me, save God's and my own;
And the hush of my heart is the stillness
   That lingers where angels have flown.

Long ago was I weary of voices
   Whose music my heart could not win;
Long ago was I weary of noises
   That fretted my soul with their din;
Long ago was I weary of places
   Where I met but the human and sin.

I toiled on, heart-tired of the human,
   I moaned 'mid the mazes of men,
Till I knelt, long ago, at an altar,
   And heard a Voice call me; since then
I walked down the Valley of Silence
   That lies far beyond mortal ken.

Do you ask what I found in the Valley?
   'T is my trysting-place with the Divine.
When I fell at the feet of the holy,
   And about me the Voice said, ' Be mine,'

Upon My Watch-Tower

There arose from the depths of my spirit
An echo, ' My heart shall be Thine ! '

Do you ask how I live in the Valley?
   I weep, and I dream, and I pray ;
But my tears are as sweet as the dewdrops
   That fall on the roses of May ;
And my prayer, like a perfume from censer,
   Ascendeth to God night and day.

Far out on the deep there are billows
   That never shall break on the beach ;
And I have heard songs in the silence
   That never shall float into speech ;
And I have had dreams in the Valley
   Too lofty for language to reach.

And I have seen thoughts in the Valley—
   Ah me ! how my spirit was stirred ;
And they wear holy veils on their faces,
   Their footsteps can never be heard ;
They pass through the Valley like virgins,
   Too pure for the touch of a word.

Do you ask me the place of the Valley,
   Ye hearts that are harrowed by care ?
It lieth afar between mountains,
   And God and His angels are there ;
And one is the dark mount of sorrow,
   The other the bright mount of prayer.

Selected.

December

All the Way

And thou shalt remember all the way which the Lord thy God hath led thee these forty years in the wilderness, to humble thee, and to prove thee, to know what was in thine heart, whether thou wouldest keep His commandments, or no.—Deuteronomy 8: 2.

IF some great event has come into our life during the past year which has changed the whole current of our being, we find it easy perhaps to recognize this as " providential." We speak of it as a direct " leading " ; especially are we ready to say so if the happening has been something pleasant. But great events are with all of us exceptional. Most lives run with the monotony of the weaver's thread—in and out, in and out, and we

All the Way

must remember that there is meaning in the monotony. By this steady movement strong and beautiful fabrics are woven, and by the " daily round, the common task," your character and mine—character in which we shall be clothed forever—has been made; and this is a fabric of value far exceeding that of the richest garments ever woven in finest looms for earthly kings and queens.

Do you think then, as you stand on the outer edge of a new year and look back over the way you have come, that this commonplace, every-day life of yours, without a single event that you would think worthy of record, has been a matter of course, without the direct and personal supervision of God?

When you look at a landscape, you notice the points that stand out distinctly: that hill yonder, that tree, those rich fields lying under the soft sky. But what is it that gives character and beauty to it all? The little things which you fail to see in detail until your attention is called to them: the blades of grass, the clusters of shrubs, the leaves. How bare it would all be, and meaningless, if these little things were not there to make each its own part of the harmonious whole! So in looking back over the year just closing, if we could read our lives aright, we would see the little things have been full of interest and serious significance.

"Thou shalt remember *all the way* which the Lord thy God hath led thee." Ah! if He has really led, then there is not so much place for regret as for thanksgiving—is there? And from the past, we may gather hope for the coming days, because this God is our God forever; He will be our guide even unto death.—Psalm 48: 14.

"Let memory walk with God through our past." To walk alone with memory

All the Way

might be so sad we could not bear it; it would be better to forget. The sin, the sorrow, the disappointment, would take away courage for the future. For the inexorable seal upon each year as it closes is, "What I have written I have written"; nothing can change the record. But if memory walks with God through our past, every spot is hallowed, every experience a memorial of His guiding, shielding, forgiving, comforting love and care.

And now, dear friend, do you question whether God really has led you, and are you grieving over "mistakes," "misfits," and things that "ought to have been different"? And do you think that your life in its minutiæ is too small for His notice? Did you ever see a mother or father—real ones, in heart as well as in name—who had so many children that they did not care for the comfort of even the least little one in the group ? Let me read what our Heavenly Father says of His interest in and care for us. In the first place He says we belong to Him.

Know ye that the Lord He is God: it is He that hath made us, and not we ourselves; [or, His we are] we are His people and the sheep of His pasture.—Psalm 100: 3.

There seems to be a sort of throwing the responsibility of us upon Him in these words. Very reverently we say it. We did not bring ourselves into this world, nor did we come here by chance. He who put us here by every consideration is bound to be interested in all that concerns us. Again and again He assures us that it is so.

The Lord looketh from heaven; He beholdeth all the sons of men. From the place of His habitation He looketh upon all the inhabitants of the earth. He fashioneth their hearts alike; He con-

All the Way 267

sidereth all their works.—Psalm 33 : 13, 15.

The variety in human faces is a wonderful thing. In all the millions upon earth, past or present, no two are exactly alike. Only the infinite mind could conceive such variety. It is so because each one is a personality, and is never lost in the multitude in God's sight. But there is one thing in which He made us the same: that is our hearts. "He fashioneth their hearts alike," so that when I bring to you the comfort of His Word which is so sweet to me, I know it will be sweet to you, and I know by my own heart's need just what this poor, tired, hungry world needs. Never forget that hearts among the Hottentots even, are made like yours, and when you share with them your Christian light and knowledge, you will see the likeness plainly.

Are not five sparrows sold for two farthings, and not one of them is forgotten before God? But even the very hairs of your head are all numbered. Fear not, therefore, ye are of more value than many sparrows.—Luke 12:6, 7.

More value! Oh, if we could see of what immense value every immortal soul is to God, we would never doubt that He thinks the least of us, and that the least thing that concerns us, is of vast importance to Him! What we need most, you and I, and all this great mass of humanity in this busy, turbulent world, is to get a persuasion of God as He sees us. How it would lift up from stupidity, despair, hopelessness, many a one who sits listlessly in the parks, or wanders aimlessly through the streets, or pursues wearily the daily toil, if once this lesson of the sparrows could find its way into their consciousness!

"Isn't it very cold for you, my little fellow?" said a gentleman, kindly, as he slipped a coin into the hand of the little newsboy. "It was cold, sir, until

All the Way

you came and spoke to me," he replied. One thought of loving-kindness brought warmth into the forlorn little soul, and even made the shivering body feel warmer. What would the thought of God's loving-kindness do for humanity? What shall it do for us these closing days of the year?

A ragged child was playing in the street on a cold winter day, when the sun suddenly burst from behind the clouds. Throwing her arms around her own half-frozen little self, looking up in the sky with a beaming face, she said, " O you dear, dear sun, shine on me lots!" So may the dear, dear face of God shine on us every day.

But the larger part of humanity is where it cannot get this view of God. Men " sit in darkness and in the shadow of death, being bound in affliction and iron." Not only in the lands of heathen ignorance is it so, but right here where the true light shineth. It is pitiful to see one sitting in the full daylight, yet thinking it is night, because sight is gone. Jesus said, " I am come a light into the world," but because light is of no use to blind people, He also said He came " to open the eyes of the blind." This is humanity's need, to feel the touch of Jesus opening their spiritual eyes to see God. And the need is being met, slowly indeed it seems, yet surely. God never was so universally recognized in human consciousness as now. We who think we know Him well may learn lessons for our profit from many who have found Him under less favorable circumstances. The recognition of God in the circumstances of their life, which one meets in visiting poor and obscure people, is very touching and beautiful.

Christians are coming to a clearer view of God. They apprehend in a broader and truer sense than formerly that His tabernacle is among men, and He dwells among them. To see God clearly ourselves, and then to make others see Him, is the highest aim that can be set before us. "Blessed are the pure in heart; for they shall see God." That pure, sincere, simple, childlike spirit which sees Him in everything is a possession most precious in itself; and when added to a pure heart gives us the power to help others secure the same treasure. How greatly is this to be desired! Humanity's cry for the Father is to be met by those who see and know Him; by those who out of forgiven and cleansed hearts say under all the experiences of life, "O give thanks unto the Lord, for He is good: for His mercy endureth forever," and who can, with the ring of happy personal knowledge in their tones, say to every downcast fellow-mortal: "Hope thou in God, for I shall yet praise Him who is the health of my countenance and my God."

But you say God has led and has cared

for those who were willing to be led—the people who asked Him. I chose to go alone, and I believe He did leave me to myself.

Well, what sort of people were these to whom He said: " Thou shalt remember all the way the Lord thy God hath led thee " ?

They soon forgot His works ; they waited not for His counsel; but lusted exceedingly, and tempted God in the desert.—Psalm 106: 13.

They were so disobedient that He said of them, as doubtless He says of us often: O that they were wise! O that my people had hearkened unto me ! then had their peace been as a river, and their righteousness as the waves of the sea.—Isaiah 48: 18.

Notwithstanding their rebellion, He led them about ; He instructed them ; He kept them as the apple of His eye.—Deuteronomy 32: 10. So we must not

All the Way

rob ourselves of the comfort of knowing He has guided though we were not always willing to be led. He has directed all.

For He maketh sore, and bindeth up; He woundeth, and His hands make whole.—Job 5:18.

Thou which hast shewed me great and sore troubles, shalt quicken me again, and bring me up again from the depths of the earth. Thou shalt increase my greatness, and comfort me on every side.—Psalm 71: 20, 21.

In the day of prosperity be joyful, but in the day of adversity consider: God also hath set the one over against the other.—Ecclesiastes 7: 14.

He can, and does, overrule for good even our mistakes, and the mistakes of others. Now therefore be not grieved, nor angry with yourselves, that ye sold me hither: for God did send me before you to preserve life. For these two years hath famine been in the land: and yet there are five years, in the which there shall neither be earing nor harvest. And God sent me before you to preserve you a posterity in the earth, and to save your lives by a great deliverance.—Genesis 45: 5–7. At my first answer no man stood with me, but all men forsook me: I pray God that it may not be laid to their charge. Notwithstanding the Lord stood with me, and strengthened me; that by me the preaching might be fully known, and that all the Gentiles might hear. And the Lord shall deliver me from every evil work, and will preserve me unto His heavenly kingdom: to whom be glory for ever and ever.—2 Timothy 4: 16–18. The Lord knoweth how to deliver the godly out of temptation, and to reserve the unjust unto the day of judgment to be punished.—2 Peter 2:9. The Lord shall preserve thee from all evil: He shall preserve thy soul.—Psalm 121:7.

He has often turned the hearts of others favorably toward us.

The Lord was with Joseph, and shewed him mercy, and gave him favor in the sight of the keeper of the prison.—Genesis 39:21. And the patriarchs, moved with envy, sold Joseph into Egypt: but God was with him, and delivered him out of all his afflictions, and gave him favor and wisdom in the sight of Pharaoh king of Egypt; and he made him governor over Egypt and all his house.—Acts 7:9, 10.

When a man's ways please the Lord He maketh even his enemies to be at peace with him.- Proverbs 16:7.

All the way? In the sorrows, the disappointments? In that grievous thing which seems so utterly against His will? Well, surely, if ever we needed His guidance and care, it was when we were in places that were dark and where we knew not which way to turn.

And I will bring the blind by a way that they know not; I will lead them in paths that they have not known: I will make darkness light before them, and crooked things straight. These things will I do unto them, and not forsake them.—Isaiah 42:16.

Through discipline, for a purpose. He humbled thee.—Deuteronomy 8:3. So then that cut I received from one I thought my friend was not an accident? It was to prove me. Could I pray for that woman? That failure I made when I attempted some work for Him—was it part of His plan, and did He "suffer" it for a purpose?

If I knew something of your every-day life through the year, how I might show you in the light of the Word how the little vexations and humblings have been known and cared about and used for your good by God. I "suffered thee to hunger." Perhaps there has not been physical hunger for any one of us; but heart hunger—ah, yes, plenty of that! There are so many things we would have been glad to have. So much that is desirable, really, that has been denied us. But it was not by chance. How it helps to know this! He suffered thee to hunger. He, who had everything at His command, and could have given everything we wanted; yet He suffered us to hunger. How could He? Because He had something so much better to give us than the thing we so much wished for. "That He might make thee know that man doth not live by bread only, but by every word that proceedeth out of the mouth of the Lord doth man live."

O wonderful lesson! A man's life consisteth not in the abundance of the things which he possesseth. I saw a child surrounded by toys at Christmas, his hands full, his lap full, he could not hold half, and he was crying because some little thing had been denied him. I have seen older people with the same spirit.

"That He might make thee know." It is difficult to make us know. It is a fact that we cannot live spiritually on the sort of food we naturally, or unnaturally, crave. And we must learn that fact somehow, or we will surely starve to death. We must find out that the things we are accustomed to feed upon do not, and cannot, give nourishment; we must be fed upon something higher and better. To find this out is the greatest discovery one can make. A little baby was failing in strength; it seemed as if it must die. " Your child is not nourished by the food it eats," said a wise doctor. A change of food was made and the baby grew and thrived. It was a great thing that the mother found that out. It may be God sees that a change of spiritual food is necessary for you if your soul shall live.

You have thought life consisted in the abundance of the "things" you possessed; you have had everything earth could give you, but you were starving; and while you possessed these things you would eat nothing better, so God took them away to show you how really famishing you were.

The thing which most nearly satisfies the heart outside of God, is human love. You thought you could "live" on that. But you could not, and God caused you to hunger—O what hunger!—by taking away the one you best loved. Our Heavenly Father knoweth that we have need of food and raiment and earthly companionships; they are His good gifts and are greatly to be valued.

But He knows that we cannot live spiritually by any of these things, and through the loss of them He makes us to know it too. Yes, *we live* by every word of the Lord,—triumphantly, hopefully, eternally live! Earthly possessions may all be gone; the circle of friends on earth may have grown very small; the hands are empty, but the springs of life within the soul are richer, fuller, sweeter than words can tell. No one can say what life is. Plants grow because they have life; we can only state the fact, never explain it. The child leaps and laughs and plays because it is "full of life." The soul soars Godward, victorious, rejoicing, because it lives! It is fed by hidden manna, and living fountains of waters. It is worth while to be made to hunger that we may find out what life truly is.

I could take you to many a home where this truth, that man does not live by bread alone, is exemplified. There is wealth, comfort, luxury,—and heartache that is killing the body. Souls are loveless, hopeless, dying, when life is apparently so full! I could take you to other homes, where the hands are weary with toil, and the head aches with planning for the family needs, and yet where the heart is rich in faith, hope, sweet Christian patience, and courage. For the lesson is twofold. It would be pitiful indeed to make us know only that we cannot live by bread; we might give up then, and say there is nothing left for us but death. But there is the positive side. By " every word of the Lord doth man live." I am come that they might have life, and that they might have it more abundantly.—John 10: 10.

I saw a beautiful child held high in the hand of her tall, strong father. It seemed so perilous I trembled lest the little one should fall. " Who's got you ? " asked her father. Without a shade of fear, with a merry laugh of delight, the baby said, " Papa! " So safe, so sure, so happy, even in a place of apparent danger, because her father held her there!

O for the simple faith of a child! In theory we do believe God holds us in His hand, and that all our ways are directed by Him; but how often in our real life do we doubt it, especially in hours of greatest need!

"My times are in Thy hand"—what a pillow for your weary head, my friend, is this! Your head, tired with regrets, disappointments, failures, mistakes of the days gone by; weary with plans and, perhaps, forebodings for the future, what a resting-place for you is here! Think of that past which you so wish might have been different; what will you do with it? You cannot alter anything now; what is written is written. But if you carry it with you into the new year it will weigh you down so heavily that you will make sorry progress. The only disposal of it is to leave it in the hand that controls all the forces of the universe, material and spiritual. The hand which fashioned many beautiful worlds out of nothing can make something beautiful for you out of mistakes and failures if He chooses; and He will choose to do it if it is best for you. It is safe to leave it all with Him and go unburdened into the opportunities of the future. "The heavens and the earth shall shake, but the Lord will be the hope [or the place of repair, or harbor] of His people, and the strength of the children of Israel." Broken and disabled, we can put in here for repairs, and then sail out upon the unknown sea courageously.

The future, with its questionings, what can we do about it? Jesus said if we should think and think forever we could not add one cubit to our stature; and if we cannot do the thing which is least, why should we be carefully anxious about greater things concerning our wellbeing, as if we had the whole matter in our own hands?

"God holds the key of the unknown, and I am glad." My times, my circumstances, my opportunities, my training, my discipline, the answer to my prayers, all that concerns me, are in His hand.

When David said, long ago, "My times are in Thy hand," he was full of trouble. His was a human heart, just like our own. He was a sinful man, a repentant man, a forgiven man, a trusting man. His faith was not perfect, for he said in his haste, "I am cut off from before Thine eyes." He thought sometimes that God had forgotten him. But even when his faith was small God heard the voice of his supplications when he cried unto Him. He is the Lord; He changeth not. He will hear us also. Even though we have not honored Him with that unvarying faith which is His due, we may confidently say: "Thou art my God. My times are in Thy hand."

The Lord thy God hath led thee—to

All the Way

bring thee into a good land.—Deuteronomy 8:7. Has He brought us there? We have tasted some of the fruits, perhaps; let us put our hand in His for another year, to be led into this good land without scarceness,—and it may be into that sweet and happy country where the humbling and hungering shall be remembered with thankful joy as a part of the way thither,

> " And this my song through endless ages,
> Jesus led me *all the way*."

RETROSPECTION.

He was better to me than all my hopes,
    He was better than all my fears ;
He made a road of my broken works,
    And a rainbow of my tears.
The billows that guarded my sea-girt path
    But carried my Lord on their crest ;
When I dwell on the days of my wilderness march
    I can lean on His love for the rest.

He emptied my hands of my treasured store,
    And His covenant love revealed,
There was not a wound in my aching heart
    But the balm of His breath hath healed.
Oh, tender and true was the chastening sore,
    In wisdom that taught and tried,
Till the soul that He sought was trusting in Him
    And nothing on earth beside.

He guided by paths that I could not see,
    By ways that I have not known,
The crooked was straight and the rough made plain,
    As I followed the Lord alone.
I praise Him still for the pleasant palms,
    And the watersprings by the way ;
For the glowing pillars of flame by night,
    And the sheltering cloud by day.

And if to warfare He calls me forth,
    He buckles my armor on ;

All the Way

He greets me with smiles, and a word of cheer,
    For battles His sword hath won ;
He wipes my brow as I droop and faint,
    He blesses my hand to toil ;
Faithful is He, as He washes my feet
    From the trace of each earthly soil.

There is light for me on the trackless wild,
    As the wonders of old I trace ;
When the God of the whole earth went before
    To search me a resting-place.
Has He changed for me ? Nay ! He changes not,
    He will bring me by some new way,
Through fire and flood, and each crafty foe,
    As safely as yesterday.

Never a watch on the dreariest halt
    But some promise of love endears ;
I read from the past, that my future shall be
    Far better than all my fears.
Like the golden pot of the wilderness bread,
    Laid up with the blossoming rod,
All safe in the ark, with the law of the Lord,
    Is the covenant care of my God.

                        ANNA SHIPTON.

www.ingramcontent.com/pod-product-compliance
Lightning Source LLC
Chambersburg PA
CBHW022116230426
43672CB00008B/1404